SHARING YOUR FAMILY HISTORY ONLINE

FAMILY HISTORY FROM PEN & SWORD BOOKS

Birth, Marriage & Death Records
The Family History Web Directory
Tracing British Battalions on the Somme
Tracing Great War Ancestors
Tracing History Through Title Deeds
Tracing Secret Service Ancestors
Tracing the Rifle Volunteers
Tracing Your Air Force Ancestors
Tracing Your Ancestors
Tracing Your Ancestors from 1066 to 1837
Tracing Your Ancestors Through Death Records –
  Second Edition
Tracing Your Ancestors through Family
  Photographs
Tracing Your Ancestors Through Letters and
  Personal Writings
Tracing Your Ancestors Using DNA
Tracing Your Ancestors Using the Census
Tracing Your Ancestors: Cambridgeshire, Essex,
  Norfolk and Suffolk
Tracing Your Aristocratic Ancestors
Tracing Your Army Ancestors
Tracing Your Army Ancestors – Third Edition
Tracing Your Birmingham Ancestors
Tracing Your Black Country Ancestors
Tracing Your Boer War Ancestors
Tracing Your British Indian Ancestors
Tracing Your Canal Ancestors
Tracing Your Channel Islands Ancestors
Tracing Your Church of England Ancestors
Tracing Your Criminal Ancestors
Tracing Your Docker Ancestors
Tracing Your East Anglian Ancestors
Tracing Your East End Ancestors
Tracing Your Family History on the Internet
Tracing Your Female Ancestors
Tracing Your First World War Ancestors
Tracing Your Freemason, Friendly Society and
  Trade Union Ancestors
Tracing Your Georgian Ancestors, 1714–1837
Tracing Your Glasgow Ancestors
Tracing Your Great War Ancestors: The Gallipoli
  Campaign
Tracing Your Great War Ancestors: The Somme

Tracing Your Great War Ancestors: Ypres
Tracing Your Huguenot Ancestors
Tracing Your Insolvent Ancestors
Tracing Your Irish Family History on the Internet
Tracing Your Jewish Ancestors
Tracing Your Jewish Ancestors – Second Edition
Tracing Your Labour Movement Ancestors
Tracing Your Legal Ancestors
Tracing Your Liverpool Ancestors
Tracing Your Liverpool Ancestors – Second
  Edition
Tracing Your London Ancestors
Tracing Your Medical Ancestors
Tracing Your Merchant Navy Ancestors
Tracing Your Northern Ancestors
Tracing Your Northern Irish Ancestors
Tracing Your Northern Irish Ancestors – Second
  Edition
Tracing Your Oxfordshire Ancestors
Tracing Your Pauper Ancestors
Tracing Your Police Ancestors
Tracing Your Potteries Ancestors
Tracing Your Pre-Victorian Ancestors
Tracing Your Prisoner of War Ancestors: The First
  World War
Tracing Your Railway Ancestors
Tracing Your Roman Catholic Ancestors
Tracing Your Royal Marine Ancestors
Tracing Your Rural Ancestors
Tracing Your Scottish Ancestry Through Church
  and State Records
Tracing Your Scottish Ancestors
Tracing Your Second World War Ancestors
Tracing Your Servant Ancestors
Tracing Your Service Women Ancestors
Tracing Your Shipbuilding Ancestors
Tracing Your Tank Ancestors
Tracing Your Textile Ancestors
Tracing Your Twentieth-Century Ancestors
Tracing Your Welsh Ancestors
Tracing Your West Country Ancestors
Tracing Your Yorkshire Ancestors
Writing Your Family History
Your Irish Ancestors

SHARING YOUR FAMILY HISTORY ONLINE

A Guide for Family Historians

CHRIS PATON

Pen & Sword
FAMILY HISTORY

First published in Great Britain in 2021 by
PEN AND SWORD FAMILY HISTORY
An imprint of
Pen & Sword Books Ltd
Yorkshire – Philadelphia

Copyright © Chris Paton 2021

ISBN 978 1 52678 029 4

Printed and bound in the UK by TJ Books Ltd, Padstow, Cornwall.

Pen & Sword Books Limited incorporates the imprints of Atlas, Archaeology, Aviation, Discovery, Family History, Fiction, History, Maritime, Military, Military Classics, Politics, Select, Transport, True Crime, Air World, Frontline Publishing, Leo Cooper, Remember When, Seaforth Publishing, The Praetorian Press, Wharncliffe Local History, Wharncliffe Transport, Wharncliffe True Crime and White Owl.

For a complete list of Pen & Sword titles please contact

PEN & SWORD BOOKS LIMITED
47 Church Street, Barnsley, South Yorkshire, S70 2AS, England
E-mail: enquiries@pen-and-sword.co.uk
Website: www.pen-and-sword.co.uk

Or

PEN AND SWORD BOOKS
1950 Lawrence Rd, Havertown, PA 19083, USA
E-mail: Uspen-and-sword@casematepublishers.com
Website: www.penandswordbooks.com

CONTENTS

INTRODUCTION

It is twenty years since I first started to research my family history as a Northern Irish born resident of Scotland. In that time I have uncovered many extraordinary ancestral stories, ranging from the absolutely hilarious to the downright tragic.

Although I commenced my research in early 2000, my ancestral background was something that I had always been curious about as a child, not least because we were the only Patons in the Northern Irish phone book. I once asked my father 'Who are the Patons?' and received the wonderfully exotic response that my grandfather Charles had been evacuated from Belgium just prior to the First World War; we must therefore have been Belgian. The whole story was somewhat vague, however, in that my grandparents had separated when my father was very young, with my Scottish-born grandmother subsequently raising her children in the County Antrim town of Carrickfergus.

Most of what my father knew about our family came from my grandmother, who had sadly long since passed away by the time I decided to take a look, but what he had been told was extremely limited. He did not know if he had any aunts and uncles, for example, nor whether he had any cousins on the Paton side. Once I started to investigate I soon discovered that my grandfather Charles did indeed have a Belgian connection, with his parents' marriage record from 1889 in Glasgow noting that my great-grandfather David Hepburn Paton was resident in Brussels at that point. However, David was originally from Blackford in Perthshire, whilst his wife Jessie hailed from Inverness.

In pursuing the story of David, his siblings and their descendants, I soon made some relevant breakthroughs. I discovered from a second cousin in Perthshire that she had old photographs of her family on holiday with a Paton cousin called 'Brussels Johnny', and not long after this I located a couple of surviving first cousins of my father in Glasgow and London. Upon meeting them, the floodgates and the photo albums opened. It transpired that my great-grandfather David had moved to Brussels to run a couple of shoe shops in the Belgian capital for a Glaswegian firm called R. & J. Dicks, which made footwear from a resin called guttapercha (from which the Scots word 'gutties' originated for synthetic rubber shoes).

Charles had three siblings: William, John (Brussels Johnny) and Annie, all of whom had been born in Belgium. Far from having been evacuated prior to the war, my grandfather had spent the entirety of the conflict as a civilian child trapped within occupied Brussels, alongside his mother and sister. His father David had been forced into hiding during the hostilities to avoid internment, and had subsequently collapsed and

The author's great-uncle John Brownlie Paton (seated), interned as a civilian prisoner of war in 1916 at Ruhleben, Germany. (See p.33)

died in a safe house in 1916. His brother John was then interned in the Ruhleben prisoner of war camp for British civilian internees for the remainder of the war (see p.33). Much of this story was corroborated in a letter from 1916 in the possession of my father's London-based cousin Joan, addressed to my grandfather's brother William, who was in Gallipoli with the Royal Army Medical Corps, as well as through photographs held by another first cousin, Anne, located in Glasgow (p.32).

Without that initial vital clue from my father about Belgium, and without tracking down and meeting our close cousins, it is highly doubtful that I would have ever learned of this epic story from the First World War involving the most immediate members of my family. And herein lies what I hope will be the equally epic point of this tale – the documents that you find in your family history pursuits will never provide the full story, and what you may already know can always be added to, enhanced and at times even transformed with the assistance of others.

The discoveries we make within our ancestral journeys can be utilised to locate further information about our family. For every fact found there will be questions raised, and other researchers and family members 'out there' may be the very folk to provide the answers. In short: it is good to share.

Twenty years ago, sharing what you might have known was not quite as easy as it is today. In the example above, written letters, car and train journeys, online discussion forums and other methods were employed to build up the picture of my family story. Nowadays we have so many more options to help us to establish contact with others who might wish to collaborate with our interests. We can present what we know online, and lure relatives to make contact through 'cousin bait', and we can proactively seek the efforts of others to try to make those connections. The very nature of the documents we can use has changed dramatically also – our very DNA can now be utilised as a primary source to encourage collaboration – but the principles of such cooperation remain the same. Share and share alike, attribute your finds, respect the privacy of the living, be courteous in your pursuits, and reap the rewards.

Whilst perhaps not quite consigned to the past yet, the days of letter writing and postcards are sadly disappearing, as the world moves further into a new digital infrastructure. Indeed, halfway through the writing of this book, our entire planet was plunged into chaos by the emergence of the coronavirus SARS-COVID-2, and the disease Covid-19, which led to an unprecedented lockdown of society as we know it. Never before have we had such a massive reliance on our online world, as governments worldwide required their populations to stay at home to try to prevent the spread of the virus, and to save lives. As I write this, digital resilience is rapidly becoming one of the key national priorities, with our children home schooling through online lessons, and with a massive increase in home working for many employees.

This raises many other important issues for posterity. How will we be remembered a century from now, if much of our contemporary documentary footprint is now digital? When the census was carried out in Scotland in 2011, for the first time we were given the choice of filling in our returns online or filling in a paper copy. I duly filled mine in online, but copied all my answers into the paper copy, which I then retained for my children, knowing full well that the official return would not be released to the public for a hundred years. In fact, I used the opportunity to record additional questions on the back of the sheet – what were my boys' favourite football teams in 2011, their favourite meals, and their favourite activities? (Never give a genealogist a blank sheet of paper...!)

Until there is a satisfactory, 100 per cent guaranteed method of digital preservation, it always pays to have a localised backup of anything you may hold dear, because despite its massive advances in recent years, the internet is still in its infancy in terms of what it can do for us.

This book will not concentrate on the online or offline documentary resources that can assist with family history research, although for those just getting started, some basic resources will be mentioned by way of a short primer in Chapter 1. For further information on available genealogical resources, please consult other works from the vast range of Pen and Sword family history titles, including my own *Tracing Your Family History on the Internet (Second Edition)*, *Tracing Your Irish Family History on the Internet (Second Edition)*, *Tracing Your Scottish Family History on the Internet*, and *Tracing Your Scottish Ancestry Through Church and State Records*.

Instead, this book will look at some of the parallel tools, resources and techniques that can allow you to make your discoveries work even harder for you, to encourage collaboration, to help you learn and to broaden the scope of your enquiries. I sincerely hope that it might provide some new ideas on how to take your interests forward to the next steps on your ancestral journey.

In producing this book, huge thanks must go to Amy Jordan at Pen and Sword for her expert assistance, to Gaynor Haliday for editing and to Tony Williams for proofreading the content, to Daniel Horowitz at MyHeritage, and to my wife Claire and sons Calum and Jamie for their ongoing support throughout, with a special nod to Calum also for his help with some of the discussion concerning social media sites in Chapter 2.

To those who have shared their finds about my family with me in the past, a further and most sincere thanks is also due – and to those who may still wish to do so, please drop me a note at **enquiry@ scotlandsgreateststory.co.uk**!

Chapter 1

RESEARCHING YOUR FAMILY HISTORY

The historic documentation that has been gathered and shared over many hundreds of years underpins the very fabric of the current genealogical world. Registers, ledgers, letters and more, recorded for a variety of purposes by institutions such as churches, the state, businesses and private landowners, all contain essential knowledge about who our forebears were and how we came to be.

Many are preserved in archives and in private collections – some may even lie in your bottom drawer, in an attic, or with your great-uncle's family overseas – whilst others may not have survived at all, presenting unique challenges to be overcome by other sources and means.

The vital records of births, marriages and deaths, for example, which can name parents, spouses, and next of kin, are only useful because of the details offered by those acting as informants to the registrars and parish clerks who took down the information offered. Where such details have been unknown or misremembered, problems will arise in research which must then be overcome from other sources and by different means. It is good to share, but we also need to be aware that sometimes facts and stories were shared incorrectly, and to compensate accordingly.

In this first chapter I will provide a broad overview of the records in the UK and Ireland that our predecessors have already shared with us, and which we rely on as a starting point in building our family trees, as well as some basic pointers to help keep you on the straight and narrow with their use.

Who, what and when?
There are many types of records that can assist with family history research; the following are some of the most common and will help you start from the present and to work your way back in time.

i) Civil registration

The state registration of births, marriages and deaths commenced in England and Wales in July 1837, in Scotland in January 1855, and in Ireland in two phases, with non-Roman Catholic marriages from April 1845, and then all births, marriages and deaths from January 1864. A General Register Office (GRO) was established for England and Wales to oversee the registration work, with separate GROs created in Scotland and Ireland. Just for good measure, the Partition of Ireland in 1921 led to the creation of a separate GRO for Northern Ireland, with the original operation in Dublin continuing the good work for the south.

In terms of establishing genealogical relationships, birth records will name both parents of a child in most cases (although earlier records will only name the fathers of illegitimate children if they were present at the registration alongside the mother), and marriage records will name the spouses and their fathers. In both cases, the couples involved, as parents and prospective spouses, were usually the informants, leading to a very high quality of information. Death records note the deceased's age at death, but rarely name a parent unless the deceased was a child. In most

The nations of the UK and Ireland have separate General Register Offices from which you can order historic birth, marriage and death records. The GRO site for England and Wales offers many records as cheap PDF files.

cases, the informant listed will usually be a relative also, and so the details provided to a registrar may not always be quite as accurate as might have been the case if the deceased had been able to do so! The exception is with Scottish records, which are considerably more detailed, noting the names of both parents to a newborn child, for marrying spouses and for the deceased, allowing you to confirm that you have the correct 'John Smith' in each record type.

The following websites are amongst the key sites offering access to the relevant records:

England and Wales	**www.gro.gov.uk/gro/content** (£)
Scotland	**www.scotlandspeople.gov.uk** (£)
Northern Ireland	**https://geni.nidirect.gov.uk** (£)
Rep. of Ireland (and N.I. pre-1922)	**www.irishgenealogy.ie** (FREE)

Free-to-access indexes for most English and Welsh records are available on FreeBMD at **www.freebmd.org.uk** (see p.63).

ii) Parish records

Prior to the advent of civil registration, the state churches in each country were the main recorders of vital records information, usually in the forms of births and baptisms, banns and marriages, and deaths and burials.

For England, Wales and Ireland, the body predominantly responsible was the Anglican Church i.e. the Church of England, the Church in Wales, and the Church of Ireland, although in Ireland the largest denomination by a country mile was in fact the Roman Catholic Church. In Scotland, the state church was the Presbyterian-based Church of Scotland.

Again, the following websites offer access to a significant proportion of such records:

England and Wales	**www.ancestry.co.uk** (£)
	www.findmypast.co.uk (£)
	www.thegenealogist.co.uk (£)
	www.familysearch.org (FREE)
	https://bmdregisters.co.uk (£)
Scotland	**www.scotlandspeople.gov.uk** (£)
	www.findmypast.co.uk (£)
Ireland	**https://registers.nli.ie** (FREE)
	www.rootsireland.ie (£)

iii) Censuses

From 1801 in Britain, and 1821 in Ireland, censuses were recorded every ten years. In 1841, the British censuses started to list names and details of everyone in a household, and from 1851 how they related to the head of that household. In Ireland, the records were considerably more detailed from the outset, but most pre-1901 Irish censuses have tragically not survived for reasons too depressing to go into here.

A one-hundred-year closure period for access means that at the time of writing the 1911 census is the most recent available across Britain and Ireland, although the 1921 census for Scotland is to be released in 2021, and for England and Wales in 2022. There was no 1921 census carried out in Ireland due to the War of Independence at that time; the 1926 census for the Irish Free State (now the Republic) will be released in 2026, although the equivalent record for Northern Ireland has sadly not survived.

Images for most census records are available on the following platforms:

England and Wales **www.ancestry.co.uk** (£)
www.findmypast.co.uk (£)
www.thegenealogist.co.uk (£)
www.myheritage.com (£)
Scotland **www.scotlandspeople.gov.uk** (£)
Ireland **www.genealogy.nationalarchives.ie** (FREE)

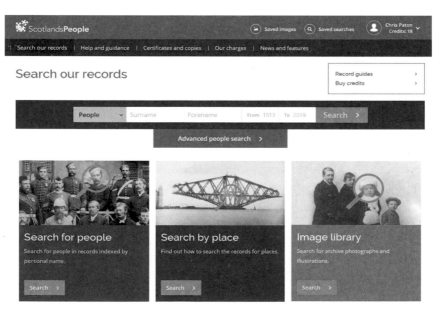

The Scottish Government's ScotlandsPeople website has historic parish records, civil registration records and censuses amongst its offerings.

Free-to-access transcripts for many records in Britain are also available on FreeCEN at **www.freecen.org.uk** (see p.63), for the 1881 Scottish census on ScotlandsPeople (p.3), and for the whole of Britain for the same year on FindmyPast.

iv) Newspapers

Newspapers are a rich resource to help understand the contemporary landscapes within which our forebears resided, and within which they may even be named, either as the subject of a reported story or as featured in the intimations columns.

The British Library's Newspaper Library at Boston Spa, Yorkshire (**www.bl.uk/visit/reading-rooms/boston-spa**), preserves an incredible range of material from across Britain and Ireland, whilst the National Library of Ireland's collections in Dublin can be identified at **www.nli.ie/en/catalogues-and-databases-printed-newspapers.aspx**.

The following sites provide digitised access to much of their holdings:

British Newspaper Archive	**www.britishnewspaperarchive.co.uk** (£)
Welsh Newspapers Online	**https://newspapers.library.wales** (FREE)
Irish Newspaper Archives	**www.irishnewsarchive.com** (£)
Isle of Man newspapers	**www.imuseum.im/newspapers** (FREE)

Genealogy vendors

In my previous internet-themed books for Pen and Sword, which were concerned with how to locate genealogical resources online for Scotland, Ireland, and the UK, I outlined many individual records collections that have been digitised by large family history-based organisations, most of which are commercial and require subscriptions, although with some free-to-access features.

In addition to carrying such records, these platforms also carry many superb additional non-records-based facilities to encourage collaboration, which will be discussed in greater detail later in this book. This includes family history software programmes and DNA testing tools.

The following are the largest such organisations relevant to British- and Irish-based research:

i) Ancestry
www.ancestry.co.uk

Ancestry.co.uk is the UK's platform for the American-based Ancestry. com corporation, which has various web domains offering access to its collections across the world. The site offers access to its digitised resources either by a monthly or annual subscription, or through a Pay As You Go model.

Ancestry is a very collaborative platform for subscribers. Not only does it invite users to help improve the standards of its transcribed indexes by encouraging corrections to be submitted, it also facilitates a massive interaction amongst its users base through its online-hosted family trees (p.72), which can help users to identify records held within its collections. In particular, its DNA platform, which will be explored later in this book (p.97), is one of the most groundbreaking tools to have hit the genealogical world within the last decade.

Ancestry also hosts a crowd sourcing facility called the World Archives Project, or WAP, which permits users to help transcribe and index much of its future content. Indexes created through the WAP become free to view upon publication, although a subscription is still required to see the actual records to which they are connected. This is discussed further on p.60.

ii) FindmyPast
www.findmypast.co.uk
FindmyPast originally started in the UK as a site offering indexes to civil registration records for English and Welsh births, marriages and deaths from 1837 onwards, and later expanded to offer British census records and parish records. Today the site has several worldwide platforms, including FindmyPast Ireland (**www.findmypast.ie**), FindmyPast Australasia (**www.findmypast.com.au**) and the US-based FindmyPast (**www.findmypast.com**).

FindmyPast very effectively engages with its readers through social media, including regular webinars (p.43) and online tutorials and lectures via Facebook (p.25). As with Ancestry, it also hosts a very effective family tree-building programme (p.78) which permits users to identify relevant records held within its databases, and to make contact with others through 'tree-to-tree hints'. At the time of writing FindmyPast has a partnership with LivingDNA (p.103), but the application of its results on the FMP platform is extremely limited.

iii) TheGenealogist
www.thegenealogist.co.uk
TheGenealogist is a platform created by Nigel and Sue Bayley as an extension of their business S&N Genealogy Ltd. As with Ancestry and FindmyPast, TheGenealogist offers many digitised and searchable British collections from the UK's National Archives and other agencies.

The company's TreeView family tree-building programme (p.80) also integrates with its records and helps users to locate prospective cousin matches, whilst the company also hosts its own volunteer transcription project (p.64). Whilst the site does have a DNA page, this is merely a sales platform for tests from FamilyTreeDNA (p.105), with TheGenealogist itself not hosting test results.

iv) MyHeritage
www.myheritage.com
MyHeritage is an Israel-based platform with some databases, which have been acquired by the company, of use for ancestral research in Britain and Ireland, although it has not initiated its own digitisation projects at archives in both regions.

MyHeritage's social media and networking tools, however, have helped to carve out a dedicated following here, most notably with its DNA platform (p.100) and family tree-based tools (p.75). As with other large online vendors, MyHeritage offers its own tutorial area to help users get the very best from its offerings.

v) FamilySearch
www.familysearch.org
Unlike the previous listed platforms, which require a paid subscription to access digitised content, FamilySearch is a free online records platform created by the Church of Jesus Christ of Latter-day Saints. Although the site has partnered with Ancestry and FindmyPast on many digitisation and indexing projects, it has a very different motivation for its efforts, encouraging users to research their family history for theological objectives as laid down by its church.

The platform has a very generous approach to its work, benefiting both church members and non-members alike with free access to many records collections. However, some collections are restricted online by licensing issues, and can only be accessed by members, or by consultation within its network of family history centres, based within various temples around the world or at affiliated locations.

FamilySearch also regularly offers family history tuition tools, including online webinars and classes (p.44), and hosts a powerful FamilySearch wiki site at **www.familysearch.org/wiki**, which encourages collaboration from its users (p.67).

One thing to note when subscribing to the large genealogy sites is that you may receive quite a few emails from them, as they try to keep you engaged with their offerings on a regular basis. In particular, if you add information from your family tree, they will try to locate matches in their records and notify you of possible research leads – these can be both a godsend and a nuisance! You may choose to ignore them, but from time to time something extraordinary may well be revealed by such a match.

When I first started to carry out my ancestral research in the early 2000s, for example, I tried to locate any possible graves which may have existed for family members in Glasgow. On my father's side I contacted the relevant burials department at Glasgow City Council, and was told that my father's grandparents had been buried in the Eastern Necropolis within the city, but that no headstone existed for them.

Some twenty years later, however, I was astonished to receive an email from MyHeritage claiming that they had a record match from their partner site, BillionGraves.com (p.65), showing a headstone for my great-grandparents and their son. When I followed this up, I discovered that there was indeed a headstone for them – they had actually been buried at Riddrie Park Cemetery, and not at the Eastern Necropolis.

Quite apart from reinforcing the need to always be able to consult original records yourself, where possible, this also illustrates that from time to time, such tools can actually create a lead, and not just respond to a request from you. I would never have gone looking for this headstone again, for the simple fact I had already been told (erroneously) that no such memorial existed.

The record on Billion Graves.com (p.65) showing the grave of author's great-grandparents in Glasgow, with their son. The record was flagged up by MyHeritage.com.

Archives

Whilst the previously noted online genealogy record vendors and suppliers offer access to digitised and transcribed records, their available offerings pale into insignificance compared with what can be sourced from archives across the UK and Ireland.

There are many national archives across the UK and Ireland, and the national library for Wales, with each presenting records online through their own platforms or through partner sites. Equally important, however, is the fact that they each share 'how to' guides describing various record types from their territories, with details on how to access them both online or offline.

The key national repositories in each country are as follows:

National Archives
   (England and Wales, also UK)   **www.nationalarchives.gov.uk**
National Library of Wales   **www.llgc.org.uk**
National Records of Scotland   **www.nrscotland.gov.uk**
Public Record Office of
   Northern Ireland   **https://nidirect.gov.uk/proni**
National Archives of Ireland   **www.nationalarchives.ie**

In addition to the national resources are local archives, university archives, libraries, and other repositories, equally overlooked at your peril.

Family history societies

If seeking advice on how to carry out family history research, a variety of family history societies exist across the UK and Ireland which can help. Societies will detail their members' research interests in their journals and/or their websites, and many will also create projects for members to collaborate on, such as the transcription of monumental inscriptions in cemeteries and graveyards, and increasingly localised DNA projects (p.105).

The umbrella organisations that most societies will belong to have websites detailing the contact details and web links for their constituent members:

Family History Federation   **www.familyhistoryfederation.com**
Association of Family History
   Societies of Wales   **www.fhswales.org.uk**
Scottish Association of Family
   History Societies   **www.safhs.org.uk**
North of Ireland Family
   History Society   **www.nifhs.org**

In addition there are societies that deal with 'one name studies', with members researching as much as they can about a particular surname, as opposed to a particular family unit, or 'one place studies', with members targeting a specific location and researching that to the fullest extent. These include:

Guild of One-Name Studies   **https://one-name.org**
The Surname Society   **https://surname-society.org**
Society of One-Place Studies   **www.one-place-studies.org**

Many societies have sharing built into their online ethos. The Families in British India Society (**www.fibis.org**), for example, has as part of its online offerings a multitude of free-to-access databases concerning Indian-based research. In addition, it also hosts a 'FibiWiki' site at **https://wiki.fibis.org**, a wiki-based platform (p.67) where users can share information useful to people researching ancestors in India.

Most societies will provide regular email-based newsletters for subscribers, with many accepting contributions for these as well as the regular journals they produce.

Genealogy magazines
Whilst there are several history and genealogy magazines servicing the UK and Ireland, two in particular have an interactive relationship with their readers.

Family Tree magazine has a website at **www.family-tree.co.uk** which includes various how-to guides and tutorials, as well as a regular newsletter.

Who Do You Think You Are? magazine carries a similar offering of tutorials and getting started guides at **www.whodoyouthinkyouaremagazine.com**.

Learning resources
There are many ways to learn about new resources for your family history research. In addition to reading the latest family history magazine editions and following genealogy blogs (p.37), most of the large vendors and some family history societies also have resources to help you develop your education. These include their online 'Help' sections, video- and text-based tutorials on their dedicated social media platforms (Chapter 2), and other resources such as live interactive webinars (p.43) where you can question staff as to their holdings and seek advice on research problems. Some dedicated interactive wiki-based tuition portals also exist, encouraging users to contribute (p.66).

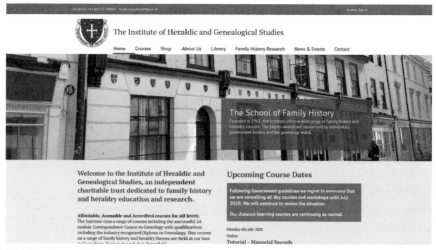

The Institute of Heraldic and Genealogical Studies is amongst many agencies offering distance learning courses for aspiring professional genealogists.

It is also possible to learn online through dedicated interactive family history courses, via short-course providers such as Pharos Teaching and Tutoring Limited (**www.pharostutors.com**) and the National Institute for Genealogical Studies (**www.genealogicalstudies.com**).

Universities offer further options for distance learning, whether at an introductory level through free to study 'massive open online course' (MOOC) short courses, or at a more formalised level through accredited undergraduate and postgraduate course, from bodies such as the University of Strathclyde: (**www.strath.ac.uk/studywithus/centreforlifelonglearning/genealogy**) and the University of Dundee: (**www.dundee.ac.uk/postgraduate/family-local-history**). The Canterbury-based Institute of Heraldic and Genealogical Studies (**www.ihgs.ac.uk**) also offers online academic tuition courses.

Good record keeping

When recording your family history it can be tempting to just note the basic details from any find and to hurtle forward to try to make the next discovery. In time, however, the sheer weight of such finds can begin to create problems if your research is not recorded correctly. You may find, for example, that you end up paying for a record again a couple of years down the line, not realising you have already found it, or you may realise one day, with horror, that you have missed some of the relevant details from a document and are unable to locate it again because you did not note where you found it in the first place.

Proving the source and credibility of your information is of vital importance when trying to convince others down the line that your conclusions are sound and based on facts. In the United States, genealogists have sought to try to codify this through what has been termed the 'Genealogical Proof Standard'. In essence this poses five challenges in gathering and interpreting information when trying to establish if a genealogical relationship can be proved:

1. Have you managed to look at as many sources as possible to back up an assertion? (What have you missed?)
2. Have you noted the provenance of any record found accurately, and in a way that may allow others to locate the same record?
3. Are the records you have located credible, and have you considered all the possible conclusions that they might suggest?
4. If there is a contradiction between sources about something you are trying to prove, have you been able to resolve that satisfactorily? (Is there still a nasty itch in your finds causing you to scratch?!)
5. Have you made a convincing argument in the way that you have interpreted your finds and written it up in a coherent way for someone else who might wish to consider the same information?

In the twenty-first-century digital world within which we now live, it is always worth bearing in mind the above questions, because the problems you will find will come thick and fast, and you may not even be aware of them if you seek to first run before you can even walk. The online world is seductive, instant, digestible; everything is just a quick click away, but sometimes you should hold back a minute or two before so doing.

One of the biggest problems you are likely to regularly encounter, for example, is the lack of source citations within online family trees, where many bold claims are made about the parentage of a particular individual with no evidence given to support such an assertion. In worst cases, absolutely bogus information may be supplied to try to lend such false claims an air of respectability and provenance. In short, for every good genealogy tree online, there is almost certainly a virtual anti-genealogy version, and if ever the two should collide it could lead to universal 'geneageddon'!

To give an example, I once had a client contact me about a family by the name of Bowes which moved from Scotland to Canada in the early nineteenth century. On various online genealogy platforms, people had repeatedly copied and pasted whole branches of this tree without bothering to check if it actually bore any resemblance to the truth. The fateful conclusion behind the original tree was that the family, being named Bowes, must have been related to the Bowes-Lyon family of Glamis, with Elizabeth Bowes-Lyon, aka the Queen Mother, being the mother of Queen Elizabeth II.

This assertion first appeared on a record within the patron submissions of the FamilySearch website, back in the day when such claims were not checked and simply added to a widely used dataset called the International Genealogical Index (IGI). It was then copied by others and eventually made its way online, with further nonsensical information added by people trying to square impossible circles. In one genius example, a marriage in the family was noted as having occurred at Inveraray Castle, despite no record shown to prove it. This was not the famous Scottish home of the Campbell family for centuries, of course, but the 'other' Inveraray Castle. There is only one Inveraray Castle, and it is well worth a visit, but the claim of a marriage there was nonsense.

Fortunately, my client did not believe a word of it, and asked me to look into the true origins of the family. By getting stuck in at the archives, I soon discovered from records not available online that the Bowes family in question was in fact from Renfrewshire, on the other side of Scotland, and had nothing whatsoever to do with the royal lineage that so many seemed so desperate to latch on to so quickly.

The takeaway line here is that if a job is worth doing, it is worth doing well. If you merely want to quickly harvest names to create a wall chart to impress folk, no-one can stop you, but if you wish to pass this on as some kind of uncorroborated legacy, you may very well be doing your posterity an injustice.

Bear in mind also that even original documents found digitised online or in an archive can be wrong. Consider the well-known baptismal record from 1704 in the parish of Ochiltree in Ayrshire, Scotland – 'George Something, lawful son of What-ye-call-him from the Mains of Barskimming'. In some cases, information may have been misheard, misunderstood, and in some cases, deliberately misreported. Documents are created by people, and mankind enjoys an epic history of screwing things up in just about every theatre imaginable. Just because information has been written down or published somewhere does not, in itself, mean that it is necessarily accurate.

There are many ways to note what you have found and where you found it. The oldest and simplest is to use a pen and paper and to keep notes through various source sheets, family group sheets, research diaries and charts. You can create your own, or download copies from the internet, such as those from Ancestry available for free at **www.ancestry. co.uk/cs/charts-and-forms**, or from FamilySearch at **www.familysearch. org/wiki/en/Genealogy_Research_Forms**.

However, you may find it considerably more to your advantage these days to purchase software that allows you to record such information on both your computer and online, which will be discussed further in Chapter 4. One key thing to note if using genealogy software is to always regularly back up your data in case of a computer failure, or even the potential future failure of the online programme hosting your information. Devices break, websites rise and fall, and technology moves on towards a digital afterlife – don't be caught out!

Privacy and data protection

If you choose to save your family tree and your research notes online, whether through a website, forum or family tree programme, be wary of the issue of privacy for relatives and contacts who are still alive.

The law offers many protections to individuals who may feel that their privacy has been breached or violated through the use of their personal data without their sanction. Most recently, the provisions of the EU's General Data Protection Regulation (GDPR) were adopted into law in the UK from May 2018, replacing the previous Data Protection Act. Through this people have a new 'right to erasure', better known as the 'the right to be forgotten', and in certain circumstances they can take action to remedy any breaches they may believe they have identified, such as identifiable data found on your public website or tree, starting with a request to you to have it removed. When the legislation was created it was not done on the basis that there would be a massive witch hunt against genealogists, it was big business and data leaks that drove the intention, but the law is the law, and it is best to be cognisant of it.

The definition of personal data by the Information Commissioner's Office (ICO) is 'information that relates to an identified or identifiable individual' and 'if it is possible to identify an individual directly from the information you are processing, then that information may be personal data'. Just for good measure, 'if information that seems to relate to a particular individual is inaccurate (i.e. it is factually incorrect or is about a different individual), the information is still personal data, as it relates to that individual'. One key thing to be aware of with data protection legislation, however, is that it only applies to the living.

As a rough rule of thumb, do not place identifiable details of people online who are still alive and/or born less than a century ago, and you

The Information Commissioner's Office has many useful resources concerning data protection and GDPR.

should be covered. Note that many archives employ a similar practice. For example, if you seek medical records from an archive, you will likely find that there will be a closure period in place for a hundred years to protect the living; in some cases a volume may simply not be provided to you, but sometimes resources can be supplied with the more recent coverage simply closed off with an elastic band, or by other means, to prevent access. Online resources will simply stop prior to the closure period kicking in.

Professional genealogists and organisations offering genealogical services should register with the ICO (**https://ico.org.uk**) as a data processor. Its guide on data protection and the GDPR is particularly useful at **https://ico.org.uk/for-organisations/guide-to-data-protection**.

Copyright and ownership

Copyright is an intellectual property right conveyed automatically to an individual upon the creation of an artistic work, and which is retained by that individual unless assigned elsewhere. There may also therefore be copyright implications for any documents or resources that you wish to share online if you have not created those materials yourself.

In most cases in the UK, the copyright on any photograph, painting, written work or music does not expire until seventy years after the death of the person who created it. If the work is published, recorded, or broadcast, there are different durations of expiry, as summarised by the UK Government at **www.gov.uk/copyright/how-long-copyright-lasts**. In addition, the Copyright, Designs and Patents Act 1988 makes a further provision for many unpublished items, extending their copyright by fifty years from the Act, to the year 2039.

For a complete overview of copyright in the UK visit **www.gov.uk/copyright**; for the law in Ireland, visit **www.irishstatutebook.ie/eli/2000/act/28/enacted/en/html**.

From a family history perspective there are a few things to be aware of on the copyright front:

i) Whilst copyright may apply to an image of a document it does not apply to the facts contained within that document, only to its visual presentation. It is therefore not a breach of copyright to extract information from a vital record certificate or a census record, for example, and to add it to a family tree presentation. Such an act, however, may separately breach an organisation's or site's terms and conditions (p.17).

ii) You may have a family photograph that you wish to put online, but if it was not created by yourself, the member of the family who took it, or the studio, will have that image protected by copyright. Whether your elderly relatives are going to prosecute you for using photos they took in the mid-twentieth century may well be an extreme reaction, but it is worth bearing in mind that they are covered legally if they wish to do so – so perhaps ask for permission first! Copyright can also be assigned or inherited.

iii) You do not actually need to place the copyright symbol © with a date on your website or work, as copyright is automatic. However, by displaying the symbol and a date you will certainly be flagging up to anyone who views it that your work is subject to copyright.

iv) There are several 'fair dealing' copyright exemptions: for example if you are reviewing or critiquing a book and wish to quote from it within your work, so long as you attribute the source. If you are using material for reasons that are not commercial, and simply for private study, this is also permitted to an extent. On this front, the UK Government guidelines at **www.gov.uk/guidance/exceptions-to-copyright# non-commercial-research-and-private-study** state that:

The purpose of this exception is to allow students and researchers to make limited copies of all types of copyright works for non-commercial research or private study. In assessing whether your use of the work is permitted or not you must assess if there is any financial impact on the copyright owner because of your use. Where the impact is not significant, the use may be acceptable.

Some materials are made available for public use online through 'open licences', such as works that have been licensed through the Creative Commons system (**https://creativecommons.org**). This allows for materials to be used in a much wider context, by defining less restrictive terms than standard copyright rules might. In addition, some materials online are actually out of copyright, and thus in the public domain. To help find out-of-copyright materials, or materials with open licences, which can be used for genealogical purposes (such as for use in blog posts), Creative Commons has a handy search tool at **https://search. creativecommons.org**.

Terms and conditions

The issue of copyright and ownership of material is separate to the terms and conditions which may be present on a platform to which you add information. On Ancestry's UK platform, for example, its terms and conditions (**www.ancestry.co.uk/cs/legal/termsandconditions**), at the time of writing, state that

You always maintain ownership of your data, but we need the ability to use your data for the purposes set out in our Privacy Statement and these Terms, and, if you agree to it, in our Informed Consent to Research.

It also adds that

As we are constantly striving to improve the Services we provide you, your data may be used to enhance our existing user experience or to develop new products and services. Unless expressly stated otherwise, each new feature that we add to the Services will also be subject to these Terms.

Ancestry further states that you can, at any time, request that it deletes your data and account. In summary, though, whilst you remain the owner of your data, in agreeing to submit your data to Ancestry's platform, it asserts a right to use it as noted above.

All major genealogy sites will have their own terms and conditions listed, and so it is always worth first consulting these before taking out a subscription to make sure that you are happy to comply with them.

Digital estate

Something you may wish to consider is what will happen to your 'digital estate' once you have passed away. This is actually a lot more complicated as a topic than may be at first thought, because you might not necessarily own the digital assets that you think you do. From a family history point of view, your digital estate might include subscriptions to websites, online-hosted family trees, digitised documents, photographs, and videos, email addresses, and cloud-based storage accounts; in a wider context it can also include PayPal accounts, banking details, and social media accounts.

If resources such as digital photographs are hosted on your own personal devices – a laptop, home computer, storage drive, phone, etc. – all should be well and good, so long as you have made arrangements to convey those devices to your nominated heir, and with any required log-in details and passwords. If your digital estate is online, however, it can get a little more complicated. Some websites have emerged in the past within the genealogy world inviting you to leave a 'digital legacy' in an account specifically designed for the passing on of your family history to the next generation, but these websites can only do so if they themselves stay in business. Can you guarantee that they will? And if not, do you have a backup plan?

Another issue is that purchases that you have made online for products do not necessarily mean that you have secured ownership, you may simply have secured a right to use it through a licence. For example, you may have purchased a subscription to a genealogy website, but simply passing on your log-in details to the next of kin after your death may actually be a breach of its terms and conditions. Similarly, if you have uploaded a photograph or a video to a social media platform, it is entirely possible that in so doing you might have conveyed a form of ownership of that version of the material to the platform itself, or granted it a specific licence, as part of its terms and conditions. You might still hold on to the copyright and intellectual property rights of such media but not necessarily anything that the company may have done with it whilst it is hosted on its platform.

In some cases, there may be a provision on a platform for a successor to take over your account. A good example is the FamilyTreeDNA platform, through which people can carry out DNA tests and store their results (see p.105). Within this site's 'Account Settings', you will find a section marked 'Beneficiary Information', into which your nominated successor's contact details can be stored. In its Privacy Statement (**www.familytreedna.com/legal/privacy-statement**) FamilyTreeDNA notes the following:

> Testers have the option to assign a beneficiary to their account in the event that they become deceased. Only in the event that FamilyTreeDNA is notified about a deceased tester, will account information be shared with the specified beneficiary. In the case that a beneficiary is not specified and upon verification of the deceased user, ownership may default to FamilyTreeDNA.

And on its 'Account Settings – Account Information' page (**https://learn.familytreedna.com/user-guide/my-account/my-account-information-page/**) it further adds:

> The beneficiary is the person who will be granted control of your myFTDNA account, your DNA test results, and any stored DNA sample in the event of your death. After they contact us, they will gain complete control of the kit and will be authorized to order additional tests with any DNA that may remain in stock.

As can be seen, in this particular example it is possible on FamilyTreeDNA for a successor to take complete ownership of your account following your passing, but if they do not, ownership of your DNA sample and your online profile will transfer to the company itself.

If you are concerned about what to do about your digital estate following death, consider seeking the assistance of a solicitor to create a 'digital will', to outline how you might wish for your accounts and data to be transferred to a beneficiary or beneficiaries.

Online etiquette

In addition to being aware about the rules and regulations surrounding copyright, and terms and conditions, there is also an unwritten code well worth following when working online. If you see an image of a relative on someone's family history website, or information about a branch of your family tree, please do not just lift it and unthinkingly integrate it into your own web based content – ask for permission to use it!

Not only will it be likely that the recipient of your enquiry will be delighted to hear from you, you might just find that what they have placed online is only a drop in the ocean compared to what they did not. Offer to share information of your own, and if permission is granted, acknowledge the source in return.

It really is nice to be nice!

Chapter 2

COMMUNICATION AND SOCIAL MEDIA

One of the most useful aspects of the online world is the ability it has given us to communicate with one another, in a variety of extraordinary ways. At the most basic level we can correspond with each other by email, but we can also proactively chat with each other in real time through social media platforms, even when on the move. In addition we can create websites to host our research on, to lure others into discovering our findings, and we can attend classes within virtual environments and learn about our shared interests together, no matter where we may be based in the world. Just for good measure, if we cannot attend a live session, we can watch a recording at a more convenient time.

In this chapter I will discuss the many ways that we can now communicate with one another for our family history research, and how we can use some of our research online to draw others to our personal cause.

Contacting relatives

Discovering new-found relatives online can be a wonderful moment but attempts to establish contact should initially adopt a note of caution. You may well be brimming with enthusiasm about researching your family, but some of your relatives may not be. They may have stories that they do not wish to share, certainly with a complete stranger, and there could well be skeletons lurking in the closet which they might wish to keep there. Worst still – and do brace yourself for this possibility – they could be completely uninterested. (I know, I am as shocked as you are!) On the other hand, there will be folk out there only too happy to hear from you. Some will have a mild interest in your approach, others will be delighted and even grateful that you made contact, as you may well fill in gaps to stories that they were already somewhat familiar with.

Up front, however, you really do not know how you will be received, so it pays to be polite and not too pushy. It may be worth simply starting with a short message, identifying who you are, how you believe you are connected, and how you hope they might be able to assist, rather than sending the entire family history across twenty volumes, especially if they only connect to a small part of it.

An offer to reciprocate with family stories may well be appreciated, and a small carrot of information to dangle in front of them by way of cousin bait may further help to lure their interest.

Email

Email is such an everyday part of our lives now that it may almost seem old-fashioned within the relatively short history of the internet, but it remains one of the most important means for communication.

For much of its early existence, emails were items that you digitally received and stored on your computer. Today, email platforms tend to be 'cloud'-based (p.55), with all your data stored on vast servers by host companies offering the service. The distinct advantage of this is that you can now access emails when on the move by simply logging into your account using your phone or laptop, as well as back at home on your computer. You can still download files that are attached for use on your devices, without clogging up the limits of your physical storage capability.

There are a variety of free email platforms available, such as Microsoft Outlook (**https://outlook.live.com**) and Google's Gmail (**https://mail. google.com**), whilst many internet providers will also provide accounts as part of your subscription package.

Whilst you may wish to have just a single domestic email account, there could be an advantage to having separate accounts for use when registering for genealogical services, and indeed, for carrying out genealogical research. For example, many companies will send regular updates and promotional material, which you might wish to avoid receiving in your normal day to day communications on your primary or work-based email addresses.

If you receive a lot of emails, a useful tip is to set up folders into which you can store messages of interest, rather than clogging up your inbox – for example, if your email account is specifically for genealogical research purposes, you might wish to create individual folders for the various surnames that you are researching.

Note that in any account that you might operate, you may receive responses that find their way into your 'Junk' or 'Spam' folder by mistake, meaning that it is well worth regularly checking such folders to be safe you have not missed a response to an enquiry.

Discussion forums

One of the simplest and often the most effective means to seek an answer to a research question, or to help others with theirs, is to participate in an online discussion forum. Not only can many people engage on a particular topic and offer advice, the conversations are preserved and made readily accessible, making it possible to search through historic enquiries and to seek an answer to a problem that may have previously been discussed by others many years ago.

The RootsChat platform at **www.rootschat.com** is probably the best known of such sites in the UK and Ireland, with well over 6 million posts and over a quarter of a million users. Within the site there are dedicated sections covering a variety of topics including the armed forces, DNA testing, the individual countries of the UK and Ireland (Northern Ireland and the Republic of Ireland are covered in a single board), and elsewhere around the world. Access is free, requiring a simple registration.

Once you are logged in, a help section readily provides guidance on how to make and reply to posts, and how to contact people using the site's internal messaging system. The forum also has a search facility that

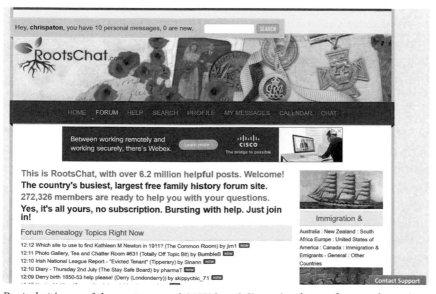

Rootschat is one of the most successful UK based discussion forums for genealogy.

allows users to make keyword searches for the name of a family or an area of interest, to help narrow down the possible historic discussions which may be available.

Elsewhere, Ancestry's RootsWeb platform is one of the oldest forums around, having been first established in 1993. It hosts some 25 million posts on topics hosted on almost 200,000 separate message boards, accessible at **https://home.rootsweb.com** or through Ancestry's home page under the 'Help' topic. There are various ways to locate boards of potential interest, including a keyword search facility, and searches for boards by surname or by locality.

For Scotland, TalkingScot offers a free-to-access dedicated Scottish-based discussion platform at **www.talkingscot.com**. The home page of the site is well worth bookmarking, as it offers a range of useful resources, including lists of family history societies active in Scotland, libraries, and a useful section on Scotland's censuses. The main forum itself has four main discussion areas, the key sections being the 'TalkingScot Forum' and 'Scots Abroad'.

A separate offering entitled Who When Where Genealogy is also available at **www.whowhenwheregenealogy.org.uk**. Amongst the topic areas under discussion on this are General Research Queries, Military, Photos, Genealogy Chat, Useful Resources, and Member Suggestions, again accessible upon free registration.

Other forums which exist include those run by family history societies (p.9) which have dedicated areas for members to discuss their interests. On military matters, one of the best resources is the Great War Forum at **www.greatwarforum.org**, which covers just about every topic that you may wish to discuss for the First World War, with many military historians only too happy to assist with enquiries.

Social media platforms

There are several social media platforms online that allow us to communicate instantly with one another, to exchange messages, links to websites, photographs, music and embedded video clips. Social media, as well as carrying messages, can also be used to quickly push content from a blog (p.37) or website (p.116), many of which will now host a small menu with links to key platforms, to allow you to share links immediately to a wider network.

One aspect to be aware of, however, when signing up to social networking platforms is that they are not charities, but businesses. When you add information about yourself to a site, it can be used to 'profile' you as a means to push specific forms of advertising your way.

By clicking on the various ads that might appear, income is generated for the firms hosting them, and you will find on many platforms a prevalence of 'clickbait' – essentially posts with links that are designed to raise your interest so that you click on them to find further content. You can also play at that game, of course! Whether you should sign up to a particular site is a decision you might certainly wish to reflect upon, but the purpose of this chapter is merely to explain how such sites can help should you choose to do so.

Each social media platform can be accessed via a web-based browser, but for smartphones and tablets you will also be able to download a free mobile 'app' (short for application); a piece of software that allows the platform to communicate directly with its subscriber, rather than through a browser. On some platforms, there is more functionality using the available app than accessing the site from a desktop browser.

The following are some of the more popular social media platforms, with suggestions as to how they might assist with your research.

i) Facebook
www.facebook.com

Facebook is a social media and networking platform which first opened to the public in 2006, and which today forms one of the most important communications platforms for individuals, businesses, archives, libraries and family history societies alike. It is technically what is known as a 'micro-blogging' platform, designed to allow users to post short text-based updates, but with added media-based enhancements.

There are many ways that Facebook can assist with research. Users can proactively search for family members to help with ancestral research, and once connected, share conversations and documents with them through the site's messenger application. You can share images on a post and 'tag' people who might be included, which will alert them to their inclusion and perhaps elicit a response. You can also join communities and pages and have conversations with experts and like-minded enthusiasts about aspects of your research.

Registration for a personal account is completely free, and requires you to simply sign up with your email address and password, your first and last name, and your birthday. Once you have a basic account you can customise your page further by adding a profile picture and a cover photo, and additional information, if you wish, in the 'About' section. Having created a basic account, you can then invite friends and family to connect to you, and establish a personal network.

The main way to communicate on Facebook historically has been through the ability to write posts, which can then be seen on the timeline of those to whom you are connected, and to which they can respond, either by a written comment, by sharing, or by giving it a 'like' to show appreciation. Indeed, today you can go beyond a simple like and respond by adding a short icon called an 'emoji', which indicates a particular emotional response you might wish to convey (one thing you cannot do is 'dislike' a post though!). When writing posts on your page, you can change the privacy setting for each post to make what you have written publicly accessible, or you can restrict it to be read only by your select group of friends or a family group.

You can categorise your followers into lists, but one particularly useful function is the ability to create a 'Family' list. To do this, visit the 'About' page and in this select 'Family and Relationships'. After clicking on 'Add a family member', type in the name of a relative and then choose their relationship to you from the drop-down menu. After you click on 'Save changes' a message will be sent to that person to confirm the connection. Once you have a populated list of family members, you can create posts specifically for them to read only.

Another very useful thing that can be created on a Facebook page is a photo album, into which you can place images for sharing and even add video clips with other family members, which can be used to encourage discussion. People can often be very passive, however, and may simply visit an album briefly and hit the like button on particular images, before moving on to the next item of interest in their timeline. To get more out of such images, it often helps to pose questions in the descriptions beneath them. Where was this taken? Who is that beside Auntie Jen? Whose wedding was this?

An album has the benefit of keeping all related images together, but it may also be worth posting images separately, one by one, over a period of time on your main timeline, and focusing the topic of discussion with each on a single event. And if you are following someone, and see an image on their timeline that you know involves a particular person, you can tag it with their name to flag it up for them to take a look at.

In addition to establishing a personal profile, Facebook allows for the creation of community pages and groups, which have different purposes. A community page allows several users to form an online community around a particular organisation or brand – so, for example, Ancestry's UK platform has a community page at **www.facebook.com/ AncestryUK**. A group, by contrast, is an area where a shared interest can be pursued, and for which you have to request access to join. Two useful

Many genealogy companies such as Ancestry, as well as other organisations and individuals, have Facebook pages on which you can find research help, news on offers, and other resources.

examples are the Genetic Genealogy Tips & Techniques group at **www. facebook.com/groups/geneticgenealogytipsandtechniques**, which is a private group for those who might wish to discuss a whole range of questions and issues relating to the use of DNA in genealogical research, and the Technology for Genealogy group at **www.facebook.com/groups/ techgen**, where you can discuss technology used for genealogical purposes, such as software, apps, tablets, computers, gadgets, news and websites. You can also create and administer such pages yourself, and invite others to help you in the task, particularly if your page becomes popular quickly and soon has a large following.

Sharing content through posts is the main way to communicate through Facebook, but it is by no means the only way. It is now possible, for example, to make a phone call or to have a video conversation with any of your friends or family based anywhere in the world, so long as they too are on Facebook and have the Messenger app installed. By visiting the 'Messages' centre on your page and selecting a person to contact, you will see options to phone or host a video conversation (see p.44). It is possible to also host a conference call and talk to several members at once – a handy way to have an online family reunion.

Another useful function on the platform is the 'Facebook Live' capability, which allows you to live stream from a location or an event, or to follow an event being broadcast. This might be a talk being given by a family history society or at a conference, a live walk-through of a new feature on a genealogy platform, or perhaps a discussion of a new records release.

One thing to be aware of is that Facebook, as with other social media platforms, regularly redesigns its platform and functionality, which can be at times extremely frustrating. Nevertheless, it remains one of the world's most popular social media platforms for a very good reason.

ii) Twitter
www.twitter.com
Twitter is another micro-blogging platform which allows users to post short text-based updates via messages of up to 280 characters in length, and which can include embedded images, videos, and GIFs (a short animated image), as well as links to website addresses, making it another very versatile platform. As with Facebook, the platform is free to sign up to, and allows users to create a basic profile page, which can include a website address, along with a profile picture and a cover photo.

Most genealogy companies and societies will have a Twitter address, with which they can quickly disseminate news announcements and themed content, with many individuals also signing up and following. The Twitter page for my Scottish GENES blog, for example, is located at **www.twitter.com/genesblog**. Twitter addresses can be shorted and searched for with a use of an @ symbol before the latter part of the URL address (p.116) – so for example, if you go to Twitter and search **@genesblog**, my page should appear. You can search for people to follow by using keywords such as genealogy and simply click the follow button to receive their content into your fast-moving timeline.

I use Twitter for many purposes, not just to share my blog content, but to learn from others about news developments relevant to ancestral research, and even to ask questions or to share finds. I have often found it easier, for example, to get a response from an online vendor through a quick Twitter exchange than by trying to contact them through email. It can also be particularly useful if planning a trip somewhere by public transport – if the train to Glasgow is cancelled for any reason, I can find out immediately and plan an alternative means to travel without having to first walk in the pouring rain to my local railway station to then receive the disappointing news!

As with Facebook, the Twitter posts, known as 'tweets', are the means of communication. If I want to mention a particular individual or group within a tweet, I simply add their Twitter address e.g. a message might say something like 'Thank you @ScotlandsPeople for the new records release', which would then be flagged up in the 'Notifications' part of the ScotlandsPeople Twitter page, for whoever is managing that account to see. I can also send a message to any of my followers through a private messaging facility.

The home page of Twitter has various menu functions, which can allow a user to find and respond to content:

Home: This link provides a page with a live feed of tweets from all of those a user is following. Tweets can be replied to, liked, or shared by 'retweeting'. You can further send a tweet via a direct message to somebody who you think may wish to see it, and you can add it to your bookmarks page.

Explore: this menu item connects to a page showing which conversations on Twitter are 'trending', i.e. which are the most popular topics of the moment, as well as topics you may wish to keep on top of yourself – for example, Genealogy.

Notifications: this links to a page showing who has liked, commented on, or retweeted any of your tweets, as well as notifying you of new followers. If someone decides to follow you, you can look at their profile and decide whether the follower is genuine (and not a spam account) – if you are not sure about whether to permit the account to follow you, it is possible to block their access so that they cannot do so.

Messages: the private messaging facility of Twitter, through which you can directly contact followers.

Bookmarks: A library area of the site into which you can save tweets of interest for further consideration.

Lists: This is a function which allows you to create specific lists of followers for a more customised reading experience, akin to a playlist.

Profile: the area of the site where you can edit your profile description and images you may wish to display.

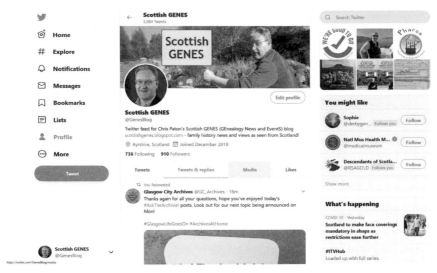

Twitter is a great way to seek advice and latest genealogy news developments.

One of the more useful aspects of a Twitter exchange is the use of 'hashtags', formed by placing the # symbol in front of a word, to highlight thematic and searchable terms, which can then be used to draw in others to a conversation. For example, when writing a tweet to promote a blog post, I will usually include #genealogy and #familyhistory at the end, so that if people search for posts on genealogy or family history using either of those terms, the list of results will include my post.

The use of hashtags can be particularly handy during themed discussion events on the platform, where all those participating can keep on top of who else is involved. A useful example in the UK is Ancestry Hour (**www.ancestryhour.co.uk**), a weekly event held at 7pm on a Tuesday evening. For the duration of an hour, anybody and everybody with an interest in family history can post anything they like, as long as it is relevant to the main theme, and so long as they tag it with #AncestryHour, inviting fellow participants to respond to posts. If you are unable to attend the session during the hour, a simple search of the term #AncestryHour will bring up all of the posts, with many fascinating tips, stories, announcements, news developments and more, all available in an easy to read digest.

Similar regular events, at the time of writing, include #ArchiveHour on the last Thursday of the month in the UK between 8 and 9pm, and #HouseHistoryHr on Thursdays in the UK at 7pm.

iii) Tumblr
www.tumblr.com

Tumblr is yet another micro-blogging platform which shares much in common with Twitter. In many ways the site is perhaps more versatile than Twitter, but it also requires a bit more of a learning curve.

Unlike Twitter, there is no limit to the number of characters permitted within a message post on Tumblr, and you can add a considerable amount more by way of media, including photos, videos and audio clips. You can also like posts that you read, and share them.

Hashtags are also permitted to help with thematic discussions, as with Twitter.

iv) LinkedIn
www.linkedin.com

LinkedIn is a social media platform for those working professionally, as well as for students or people seeking work. If working as a genealogist it is a useful place to build up a network of professional contacts from a range of useful disciplines.

A user's profile page essentially acts as a curriculum vitae, allowing information such as Experience, Education, Recommendations, and Accomplishments (within which you can display information about publications, languages spoken, etc.). Through the platform, it is possible to message other users, to display your latest activities, and to seek employment.

There is a basic free subscription option, and a Premium Subscription Plan, offering enhanced functionality.

v) Other platforms

There are plenty of other popular social media platforms out there designed for instant messaging, including Snapchat (**www.snapchat. com**) and WhatsApp (**www.whatsapp.com**).

Users of Snapchat can determine the time available for a user to read a post containing an image or a video (called a 'snap'), up to ten seconds upon being opened. It is popular with the younger generation, but as a tool for genealogy it is probably not the most useful item in the bag.

WhatsApp is a free platform owned by Facebook, on which you can create private community groups of up to 256 people within which you can discuss issues, share images and documents, and send text, voice and video-based messages. Calls will work between different iOS and Android-based devices; a further useful feature is that you can save your message history on Google Drive (p.57).

Image sharing

One of the greatest experiences that a family historian will ever enjoy is the moment when a long-lost photograph emerges depicting an ancestor or a relative. In many cases, such a discovery can transform the understanding that we may have previously constructed for a relative from our documentary sources – but it can also be fun to look for any family resemblances and traits that may have been passed down through the generations!

Whilst many genealogy platforms offer historic photograph collections, MyHeritage (p.7) has very successfully latched on to the emotional resonance and power of the family photo as a means to stimulate discussion. In 2020, the company released two new tools that have injected a great deal of fun into the use of imagery for family history research – 'Colorize photos' and 'Enhance photos'. The first is a software tool that allows users to add colour to old black and white photographs, giving them a more twenty-first-century sense of realism and immediacy, whilst the second is a tool that seeks to retrieve the features of ancestors depicted in slightly blurry photos. The net result is that for some old out-of-focus black and white images, the tools can provide a visual enhancement that makes them seem as if they were created just yesterday. Such images can then be downloaded to your computer, or sent via Facebook or Twitter to friends and relatives to stimulate further debate from their contents.

As well as providing a talking point from which memories of events can be retrieved by relatives, old family photos can also convey historic information in their own right. You may well be fortunate to come across a picture that has the identity of a person written on the back, or which holds other clues to suggest what may be happening and where. When I met my father's first cousin Anne in Glasgow for the first time, she had a bag full of old family photos that she allowed me to take copies of, some of which had information identifying who the relatives depicted were. The most exciting find was a postcard of my grandfather Charles as a child from 1907, sent from Brussels by his father to the rest of the family back in Inverness. Not only did the reverse of the card have a short message addressed to Charles' sister, partly written in French, and to the family address in Inverness, it also noted the details of the Brussels-based photography firm which had taken the picture of Charles. On the edge of the card, two studio addresses were printed matching the names of the streets on which my great-grandfather David managed his two Belgian-based shoe shops.

Another postcard, however, was much less detailed, and required further assistance online to help resolve its mystery. Although Anne knew that the image in question depicted my grandfather's brother John Brownlie Paton (her uncle), on the reverse it merely stated an address in Glasgow to which the image had been sent, and the words 'J. B. Paton Bar 4' in the space for the message. Anne knew that John had been arrested as a civilian prisoner of war in Brussels when he had reached the age of 16, but she did not know where he had been interned. Many years later, however, I traced another cousin who turned out to hold a copy of the same postcard, as posted to her branch of the family, and who kindly scanned both the front image and the reverse, which she then emailed to me. Whilst the image of John on the front was exactly the same as that on Anne's postcard, it was the back of the image that solved the puzzle about where he had been imprisoned. Unlike the first card, there was no handwritten message, there was simply a postmark which stated two words written in German – *Ruhleben Freigegeben*. This confirmed that John had been sent from Belgium to the German civilian prisoner of war camp at Ruhleben, near Berlin. This is a good example of how, when sharing postcard images online, the information on the reverse of the card, no matter how seemingly limited it may be, might still have the ability to resolve a brick wall problem – so if a distant cousin suggests there is an image available, ask for copies of both sides!

Many photographs are now born digitally, and may never be reproduced in a printed format. Even within such images, there may be

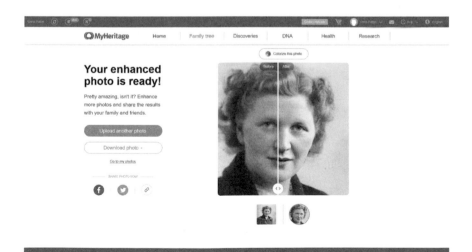

MyHeritage's Enhance photos tool, along with its Colorize photos tool, is a great way to have fun with old family photos and to encourage discussion with relatives.

hidden information embedded within them that can help with research, in the form of what is known as metadata, a word that is essentially defined as 'data about data'.

When viewing a digital image using a Windows-based home computer, for example, you can right click on an image with a mouse and in the menu that appears, select the last option, 'Properties', and then the option marked 'Description', to reveal a page of details about how the image was recorded. This can include the date and time when the picture was taken, the type of camera that was used, the settings employed by that device to do so, the image's size and resolution, and even the GPS coordinates of where the image was recorded – a capability that can be particularly useful when applied to projects that require such information, such as the photographic recording of gravestones within a cemetery (see pp.64–5).

You can also manually add additional metadata in photographs after they have been taken, through the use of the comments and tags fields within this Description menu option, and, of course, within the name of the photographic file itself. One thing to be aware of, however, is that when transferring digital images to some websites and social media platforms, such metadata may be stripped from the image when it is uploaded, and if the images are compressed in any way.

There are other tools that can assist with identifying the subjects of digital imagery. Google has a 'reverse image search' tool, for example, that allows users to upload an image, and to look for other pictures online showing the same location, or other versions of the same image, which may have accompanying information or be perhaps presented in a better resolution – in essence, the tool basically allows you to carry out a search using an image instead of a keyword. To use this tool, simply visit Google Images at **https://images.google.com** and click on the camera icon beside the search box – you will then be invited to either post a URL (p.116) of the image if already hosted online, or to upload an image.

Something to consider with digital images is the file format that you might wish to use to save them on your home computer. There are several different file formats available, but there are pros and cons to each.

By far the most commonly used file format is that of a JPEG file (with files ending in .jpg) because it produces considerably smaller file sizes than some of its competitors. Whilst this can be of real benefit in terms of storage, a downside is that JPEG files are 'lossy' documents, which means that when the image is compressed for storage, some of the quality is lost. If you repeatedly open a JPEG file and save it, you will be constantly re-compressing it and losing a little bit more of the quality each time you do so, with the process being irreversible. By contrast, 'lossless' file formats such as PNG (.png) and TIF (.tif) do not lose any quality upon repeated opening and closing, but whilst from a preservation point of view, such formats are clearly preferable, the image files are considerably larger in size. This can lead to potential storage issues, and in some cases such images may not be supported by certain online sites and platforms as a consequence.

As with text, images can be used to generate discussion, and social media platforms can be a very effective means to do so. There are several platforms available that specifically use imagery as their main currency, allowing users to upload photographs and video clips. The following are some of the more popular platforms:

i) Instagram
www.instagram.com
Instagram is a free social networking platform owned by Facebook that allows users to share photographs and videos. You can append text messages to items when posted, and as with Twitter you can use hashtags (p.30) in your messages, which can allow you to locate posts and pictures on a particular theme. Images can be taken with your device through the app whilst it is open, or you can import them from your phone or tablet gallery and post from there.

Images are viewed on a timeline, and you can like, comment on, share images using Facebook, Twitter, Messenger or email, or alternatively bookmark images that you might wish to save. To share a post, you will see an image of three vertical dots to the extreme right of the poster's name at the top; click on this to reveal a menu inviting you to copy the post's link for use in a text-based message, or to 'Share to' others via a variety of other social media options.

Although a useful way to share photos, one shortcoming with the programme is that you cannot include an active hyperlink for a website's URL (p.116) on a free account, although you can add a workable link into your profile page.

A further frustration is that you cannot easily directly download an individual image from an Instagram post, nor upload images to the platform from a desktop browser. It is possible to save all photos and videos from your Instagram account directly to your phone as a default; to do so, click on the 'Settings' menu via your profile page, then 'Account', then 'Original Posts' – you will now have an option to save original unedited images, posted photos and posted videos directly to your device.

ii) Pinterest
www.pinterest.co.uk

Pinterest is a useful free social networking platform that allows users to post or 'pin' images found online into dedicated folders or 'boards' within an account. You can follow other people's boards for topics of interest, and check in to see what images may be of interest, as well as click on links to articles that they connect to online.

On my Pinterest account, located at **www.pinterest.co.uk/chrismpaton**, I regularly pin images to specific boards which link to my genealogy news blog. Amongst the Pinterest boards I host are boards for my Scottish GENES blog, another for Irish genealogy, Scottish family history societies, genealogy magazines, English genealogy, European genealogy, and many more.

As well as helping to store stories within specific categories, they also bring in additional readers who may be attracted to a particular image before reading a headline.

iii) Flickr
www.flickr.com

Flickr is a platform which allows you to host images and videos within dedicated folders, which you can comment on and share with other interested parties. In addition to creating your own albums of images, you can also create curated 'galleries' of material found from other accounts online.

In order to make your images more easily findable, you can embed tags within them, essentially keywords that can match a useful search term. For example, if you include a photograph of a relative, not only can you add their name as a tag but perhaps also a location where the image was recorded.

At its most basic, a free Flickr account at the time of writing granted a free allocation of 1000 GB of storage, but it is also possible to pay for a pro account, which provides some additional functionality, such as 'Flickr Uploadr', which allows you to back up your photo collections from your home computer and other social media tools, such as Dropbox (p.55).

Flickr has been particularly popular amongst archivists as a means to display certain digitised image collections from their repositories. A good example lies with the Public Record Office of Northern Ireland FLICKR page at **www.flickr.com/photos/proni/**, which hosts images in a number of folders, and invites users to comment on them to try to help explain the context of what is being depicted from more local knowledge.

Blogs

Blogs are websites that encourage the regular posting of content, with the word 'blog' a contraction of the term 'web log'. In essence, they are online diary-based platforms that can be customised for a variety of purposes. Those who write blogs are often referred to as 'bloggers', and can build up a loyal following of subscribers who regularly tune into what they have written to keep up with the latest instalments.

There are many ways that blogs can be used within the genealogical world, and indeed, I keep two of my own for very different purposes. Since 2007, I have been writing a daily news blog called Scottish GENES at **https://scottishgenes.blogspot.com** (and for part of that time British GENES at **https://britishgenes.blogspot.com**), in which I share the latest news and developments in the genealogical world that I find of interest as a Scottish-based Ulsterman. Although I cover stories from across the UK and Ireland, as well as from around the world, my own personal interests are those stories which affect my research within the two countries I am most closely connected to: Scotland and Northern Ireland. Readers can subscribe and receive daily news feeds, and comment on posts, to which I can respond further.

A separate blog that I write for less frequently is one hosted on my *Scotland's Greatest Story* genealogy research service page at **https://scotlandsgreateststory.wordpress.com/blog**, in which I occasionally produce articles about types of records that I encounter in my work as a genealogist. The idea is to help provide useful articles for folk carrying out their own research, but also as a means to demonstrate (hopefully!) some ability at my end within the field that I now work.

Blogs can be used in a variety of creative ways within the genealogical and historical worlds. Many family historians use them as a means to write articles about their discoveries, very much in the style of an ongoing journal. A great example is Janet Few's blog, *The Latest News from the History Interpreter*, at **https://thehistoryinterpreter.wordpress.com/latest-news-from-the-history-interpreter**. Janet is a living history interpreter, one place study enthusiast, genealogist and author, and her blog regularly updates readers in an amusing way about her ongoing finds. On Janet's platform she states that 'Here you will find my ramblings about history, genealogy and writing, as well as accounts of my various travels hither and yon', adding that folk can also follow her on Twitter but that they should 'beware, I have no idea where I am going'. This should probably be a genealogical motto!

A blog is also a great way to write individual posts about specific ancestors, as a means to create a written family-based archive. You can post as often or as little as you like, and write entries as long or as short as you like. One of the most useful aspects of a blog is that every word you write within your post can be searched by a search engine such as Google. Say for example, you have written a piece about an ancestor called John Smyth from Springfield, Belfast, and someone else carries out a Google search for the same individual, then your blog post will likely emerge as one of the first results. As such, blogs can act as one of the greatest cousin bait traps imaginable, to lure in those prospective cousins. To benefit from their visit, however, you should make sure that when writing an entry that you have enabled a means by which your reader can interact to establish contact. You could, for example, include a website address to your dedicated family history website, or you could include a comments section into which your prospective cousin can write a response.

You could also utilise a blog for various other project-based activities, for example, to reproduce a historic diary in 'real time', by reprinting posts on the anniversary of the date on which they were first written. A wonderful example of this was a former blog entitled *Voyage of the Vampire*, sadly no longer a live website but thankfully preserved on the Internet Archive (p.117) at **https://web.archive.org/web/20141223134737/ http://www.voyageofthevampire.org.uk**.

This reproduced entries from the diary of Sir George Henry Scott Douglas in 1846, as he sailed on board the *Vampire* from Corfu to Greece and Turkey as a captain in the 34th Regiment of Foot (The Border Regiment).

Alternatively you might create a blog in which you regularly describe visits to locations relevant to your ancestry, for example to churches within your home county, and note connections you may have to them.

A useful website for locating genealogically themed blogs, which can provide inspiration for such projects, or from where you may simply find blogs of interest in their own right, is the GeneaBloggers Tribe platform at **http://geneabloggerstribe.com**. This allows bloggers to register their ancestrally themed blog into a directory, which can be searched for using a particular keyword.

For example, if I search for blogs using the term 'DNA', it flags up sixty-six separate blogs on the subject, whilst a search for a blog on the subject of surnames locates forty-three such projects. The site's 'Blog Resources' page at **http://geneabloggerstribe.com/resources** also has many useful tips on how to create blogs, and best practice for their use, as well as many articles and tips on other aspects of social media use.

There are many blogging platforms available for genealogists to use, but by far the most widely utilised by genealogists worldwide are Blogger and Wordpress.

i) Blogger

www.blogger.com

Google's Blogger platform is a very user-friendly platform which does not take long to learn how to use, and which is completely free of charge. To be able to create a Blogger-based blog, however, you need to first register for a free Google account, which can be done at **www.google.co.uk**.

If you take a look at my Scottish GENES blog at **https://scottishgenes. blogspot.com**, which is hosted on Blogger, you will get an idea about the kind of flexibility that a Blogger-based platform can offer. The latest blog posts are presented in chronological order on the page, with the most recent at the top. If I click on the title of the blog post, this opens up the post in a dedicated page of its own, and with its own URL (p.116) or website address. If I then copy this URL, I can paste it into a Facebook post, tweet, email message, or any number of other platforms, and guide people specifically to that post.

Within my posts I usually try to include an image, for the simple reason that if people follow my blog through a reader (p.43), or if I post the article on a platform such as Facebook, a small image pops up beside the blog title which can help lure somebody in to read the piece. It is

Google's Blogger platform allows you to quickly set up a fully customisable blog, which can include many pages and 'gadgets'.

very easy to upload images to a Blogger post from your computer. The images are stored in your Google album archive, and once uploaded can be used repeatedly across multiple blog posts, without having to upload the same image time and again.

You can permit readers an option to comment on a blog post, with various defences against spammers available, such as comments posts needing to be manually checked by yourself before they can be made visible.

At the bottom of each published post you will see there is a small line which states 'Labels', alongside which are listed various random words. These words or tags can be applied to any post you wish, and can help you locate any post which has been similarly tagged. On the right side of the home page, in the smaller column, you will see a section also marked Labels about halfway down, where these tags are listed in alphabetical order and with a small number in brackets after. This refers to the number of posts to be found in total on the blog which have been similarly tagged with the same label, and by clicking on the word, a list will be returned of all such articles. For example, if I click on the tag marked 'Canada', then any post that I have written which mentions Canada will be listed – a handy way to locate useful content in a blog, particularly if it hosts many posts. If you were to write a blog about individual family members, for example, you might add a label for a surname, e.g. Smith, and in time, after you have written several more posts about this line, you will easily be able to locate all of those featuring members of the Smith family.

Also in the right-hand column you will see other functions, which Blogger calls 'gadgets'. These include a facility to subscribe to a daily email feed, and various images with embedded links – in my case, providing links to vendors selling some of my books, or to genealogy groups I may be a member of. There is also a search box, which allows users to search through posts, and a chronological archive hierarchy showing the names of all my posts, which can be clicked on for immediate access. The gadgets are fully customisable from within Blogger's 'Layout' page, and completely free to add.

Whilst posts appear on the front page of a Blogger-based blog, the menu at the top of the page also shows a variety of additional pages that can be consulted, in my case with additional pages noting information about some of the services I provide, as well as some useful resources. The format of a Blogger page is fully customisable, and I could have three columns instead of two, if I wished, with a background picture behind the posts, or different font styles and different colours. To make changes to the site's look, you click on the 'Design' button at the top right side of the page, which leads to a management area for the blog.

One of the great reliefs about Blogger for me personally is that when writing a blog post, I do not have to have any experience of using the HTML computer language (p.117) – I can literally write and what I see is what I get. To create a post, simply click on 'New Post' at the top right of the page, and you will be taken to a template for a new post, which can be viewed in two ways, through the 'Compose' view or the 'HTML' view. Compose view is a basic 'what you see is what you get' page, and is brilliant for those, like me, who know next to nothing about what actually makes computers tick! However, if you are more experienced, the HTML view can be useful for specific tasks. If you write a post, for example, within which you might wish to embed a YouTube-hosted video clip (p.120), you might copy the HTML code for the clip and add it into your post in the HTML view, before switching back to the Compose view. Once the basic post is written you can publish it straightaway, or schedule it to be published at a specific time and date.

ii) Wordpress
https://wordpress.com and **https://wordpress.org**
Just as popular as Blogger is an alternative platform called Wordpress, although there are in fact two different versions through which you can host a blog or website, being Wordpress.com and Wordpress.org.

If utilising Wordpress.com, you will need to register for an account before creating your free blog on the company's dedicated platform. For basic users and beginners, this version of Wordpress takes the pain out of trying to set something up, offering a variety of templates from which you can very quickly create a dedicated site for your genealogy needs. There are a variety of themes and styles, and once you get used to the navigation around the site it becomes relatively straightforward to use. A downside of using Wordpress.com, however, is that your URL address (p.116) will include the ending '.wordpress.com', unless you upgrade to a premium plan – although an alternative is to purchase a domain name (i.e. a customised address for your site) from another provider and redirect that to your Wordpress address, if required. If you use the completely free plan, then you will also find some advertising popping up, which is another trade-off to consider.

Wordpress.com is probably the easiest platform to start with, and the site has a handy wizard guide at **https://wordpress.com/create-blog** to help you establish your blog. The site will first ask you register your site's domain, and offer you subscription-based alternatives to a domain that does not includes a .wordpress.com ending, but you can skip past these and stick with the free option. Once you have skipped through the initial sales pitches you will be presented with a basic draft blog which you can customise, by changing the theme of the site, the text and other customisable features. The basic templates can be adapted to include your own images, should those available not be to your liking.

Throughout the creation of the site, you can switch between the draft view you are working on and a 'Preview' view, which will allow you to see how the site looks on a PC, on a mobile phone and on a tablet.

As noted earlier, as a blogger I have personally opted for Google's Blogger platform to disseminate news on a daily basis, but I do also have a Wordpress.com-based website and blog for my research service, which is available at **https://scotlandsgreateststory.wordpress.com**. I have set the website up to offer several pages detailing my research services, but with a dedicated blog available on the site as a last item on the menu. I tend to use this blog more for carrying articles about various types of records or locations I have visited during activities carried out during my research, to help provide more of a flavour of the research environment within which I work. As you can see from the bottom of any post on this blog, there is an option for me to share content on to Twitter and Facebook.

Wordpress.org is an alternative for those why may have a better idea of what they are doing, and who would like a bit more control over the proceedings. For this you will need to download the free software on to your own computer and then upload whichever site you create to a dedicated server of your own choosing, for the relevant subscription fee.

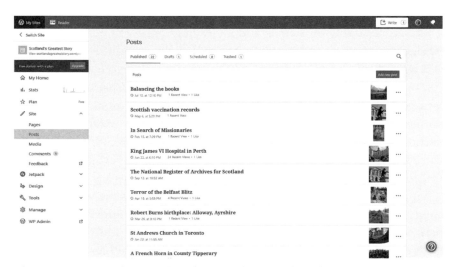

There are two types of blog platform from Wordpress, with the free to use Wordpress.com the easiest to start with.

You can also use your own domain name for your site, and there are a few more bells and whistles to help, such as a further flexibility with files and databases that you may wish to host.

One of the additional benefits of the Wordpress.org platform is that you can add 'plugins' (**https://en-gb.wordpress.org/plugins**), essentially additional pieces of software that can add further functionality to your page. Some plugins are free, whilst others require purchase. For family historians, for example, plugins for family tree-hosting on a Wordpress. org page can be located at **https://en-gb.wordpress.org/plugins/tags/ genealogy**.

Note that plugins are also available for Wordpress.com sites, but in order to install them you will need to have a Business Plan subscription.

Feed readers

There are so many genealogy blogs out there – as well as other web-based content from magazines and other sources – that it can be difficult to keep a handle on what may be of interest or of use to your own research. Many magazines will produce lists of what they deem to be some of the more interesting blogs, whilst some genealogy bloggers actually review blogs on a regular basis to curate content for their readers.

Another alternative, however, is to use a piece of software known as a 'feed reader' to gather content. The two competing standards on this front are RSS feed readers (with RSS standing for Really Simple Syndication) or Atom-based readers; the bottom line is that both will sift out the stuff that you are interested in and make them easily accessible to read.

There are many options available, but amongst the more popular readers for genealogists is Feedly (**https://feedly.com**), the free version of which allows you to receive content from up to a hundred different sources. This can be accessed on a web browser or as a downloadable app for your phone or portable device. By typing in the RSS feed addresses for sites of interest, the reader will continually provide links to the latest articles for you to easily access.

Note the RSS feed address for a site is not the same as its URL address (p.116). A useful article on how to locate the RSS feed address for a particular website is available at **https://rss.com/blog/find-rss-feed**.

Virtual meetings and webinars

Alexander Graham Bell invented the world's first telephone in 1876, and by 1915 the world's first transcontinental phone call was made. Today we can not only talk to each other on mobile phones, we can also see each other as we converse through video-based conversation platforms, with conversations involving many participants in real time. As the conversation progresses, you can share the contents of your computer screen and show materials from your home screen, for example using a PowerPoint presentation.

Indeed, during the coronavirus pandemic of 2020, the use of such video technology came fully into its own, with many family history societies having to cancel long-planned-for meetings and physical conferences, and instead switch to online platforms to hold virtual replacements in the form of 'webinars' (web-hosted seminars). For some societies, this had the added advantage of introducing new members to their proceedings, many from overseas, who would previously have only been able to participate if they had travelled to the host country.

Several platforms facilitate video-based conversations:

i) Facebook Messenger

Facebook permits free calling, both audio and video, through its Messenger or Messenger Lite app, although video chatting was not available worldwide at the time of writing. In order to make a call, participants will need to first make sure that the cameras and microphones are switched on through whichever devices are utilised.

If making a video call using a smartphone, and it has both a forward and rear facing camera, you can switch between cameras during your conversation, potentially handy if you wish to ask someone a question about something in a room or whilst out and about on location during your conversation.

To make a call, you either click on the name of the person you wish to call, or the group of people, and simply click on the video camera icon. The other participant or participants will be notified and asked to accept your call. Once done, you will see how you are portrayed in a small screen on your device, whilst an image of the other person will dominate the screen. You can mute your audio or disable your video feed at any stage during the call.

ii) Zoom
https://zoom.us

Although established in 2011, California-based Zoom Video Communications really came into its own during the coronavirus pandemic of 2020, as a major free-to-access videoconferencing tool, not only for business use, but for families who were locked down. For children who were home schooling, it was a handy means for teachers

Zoom is a superb platform for hosting conversations and family reunions online, with relatives from around the world being able to join in.

to share lessons, particularly when Zoom extended the time limit for free basic sessions for schools, whilst for many families it had the added bonus of bringing together relatives through fun activities such as weekly quizzes.

The free Basic version of Zoom permits video conferencing calls of up to forty minutes for meetings involving three or more participants, to a maximum limit of one hundred, although a meeting link can be re-used upon the session's expiry to continue the conversation, if everyone signs in again. Subscription-based options permit longer meetings up to 24 hours, with capacity for 100, 300, 500 or 1,000 participants, dependant on the selected plan.

When hosting a webinar, you can share a PowerPoint presentation with your fellow participants, or demonstrate some other activity using your computer. You can also extend the reach for those who may wish to watch by streaming the session live on either Facebook or YouTube – in so doing, a live stream to either platform counts as a single attendee to your Zoom conference. A useful video guide from Zoom on how to do this is available on YouTube at **https://youtu.be/UkX640vqozE**. Zoom sessions can also be recorded.

iii) Skype
www.skype.com
Skype is a free platform owned by Microsoft, and can be accessed through a browser using the website address above or opened within an app on a smartphone or tablet device. As well as permitting audio

or video calls, you can also send messages by text to an individual or a group. Calls between two Skype users are completely free, but you will need to pay to make calls to phones that do not host the Skype app.

Users can host a group-based audio or video conversation using Skype's 'Meet Now' function, which permits a group of up to fifty people to attend, and up to nine people can be viewed on a screen at any one time. Creating a meeting is easy: after selecting Meet Now from the calls menu item, you simply create a call link and use the facility's 'Share invite' button to invite participants to attend, whether they have a Skype account or not. The maximum length of a video call is four hours – if it continues beyond this duration, it will switch all participants to an audio call.

Note that Microsoft also has a separate paid-for-subscription feature called Microsoft Teams (**www.microsoft.com/en-gb/microsoft-365/ microsoft-teams/group-chat-software**), which offers video calling and webinar functions, but which, at the time of writing, was for professional use only.

Although there is a free trial version, when you try to register to use the service you will be asked if your intent is to do so for use 'For school', 'For friends and family' or 'For work' – if intending to use it for friends and family, Microsoft will immediately redirect you towards signing up for a Skype account instead.

iv) Facetime

Facetime is a video- and audio-based communications tool that can only be used on Apple-based products such as iPhones, iPads and Mac computers. It also facilitates group discussions, with up to thirty-two users at any one time.

To connect with somebody, you need to download the Facetime app on to your device, and then type in the recipient's phone number or email address. If making a phone call with an iPhone, you can actually switch to Facetime in the midst of it to turn it into a video-based conversation.

A guide to using the service is available at **https://support.apple.com/ en-gb/HT204380**.

v) GoToWebinar
www.gotomeeting.com/en-gb/webinar
Another popular service used widely by genealogists worldwide is GoToWebinar, part of the GoToMeeting platform.

Many family history societies use this site to host genealogical webinars and conferences with guests and speakers in attendance from around the world. Presentations can be shown using your desktop to show slide presentations or live demonstrations, and verbal question and answer sessions can be held, as well as contributions made by text.

A useful introductory video providing a flavour of the site's facilities is available at **https://youtu.be/uDdg_Z2KzHs**. GoToWebinar offers a free seven-day trial for events with up to 100 attendees, after which you will need to purchase an annual subscription to cater for 100, 500 or 1,000 attendees, as well as to provide for further facilities, such as an ability to record sessions and to offer them as pre-recorded on-demand webinars.

Chapter 3

COLLABORATION AND CROWDSOURCING

Whilst the internet provides us with a useful means to communicate with one another for research purposes, it also offers many opportunities for people to collaborate on projects of genealogical interest, and to create useful resources from a much wider effort. Our true family history and identity can only be determined from the sum of all of its parts, but for many of us those parts may well be scattered across the world.

Many opportunities exist for users to try to utilise the information they hold to generate further leads. The use of discussion forums such as Rootschat (p.23) may be one way to do this, but there are also platforms that focus on specific resources or locations that families might have in common. Indeed, one of the fastest growing areas where the internet has helped to revolutionise genealogical research in such a manner is in the use of DNA databases, which provide the means for distant relatives to determine just how much DNA that they might share with one another, as a way to promote contact and to facilitate further advances with ancestral research. DNA is such a large subject that it will be looked at in detail in Chapter 5.

In addition, technology now permits us further ways to collaborate, through the use of cloud-based storage sites, and online data platforms through which we can work together to produce further finding aids and help resources. In this chapter I will explore many of the ways that we can go about initiating such cooperation.

Collaborative platforms

The following projects are just some of those currently available for genealogists to both utilise and exploit common resources shared by other researchers to try to establish connections.

i) Lost Cousins
www.lostcousins.com
The Lost Cousins networking platform was first established in 2003 by Essex-based software developer and family historian Peter Calver. The site today has more than 90,000 members registered, and offers free registration, although a basic annual subscription (£10 at the time of writing) facilitates some additional perks (see **www.lostcousins.com/pages/members/subscription**).

The concept behind the site is deliciously simple, and acts similarly to the concept behind more recently established ancestral DNA networking platforms (see Chapter 5). Rather than adding a user's DNA profile online to lure relatives through matches, it instead utilises a very different document that is shared by prospective cousins, in the form of census records. Members are encouraged to add details of census entries within which their ancestors have been confirmed as appearing; if somebody else adds the same details for one of their ancestors, then the site flags up the match, and hey presto, you have found an instant 'lost cousin'. Once

Lost Cousins is a handy website for trying to target connections with relatives by locating common ancestors through historic censuses.

the match is established, the two connected cousins can now contact each other, and work out the rest of their shared story.

The censuses from which information can be shared on the platform are as follows:

- England & Wales 1841
- England & Wales 1881
- England & Wales 1911
- Scotland 1881
- Ireland 1911
- United States 1880
- United States 1940
- Canada 1881

Links to free access for some of these censuses are available at **www. lostcousins.com/pages/info/census_search.mhtml**, although you may also find some information for the British censuses for free via FreeCEN (p.63).

The process for sharing information is simple. On the site's 'My Ancestors' page you will be invited to add the names of known relatives and the basic source details from their census entry, which conforms to the territory within which they were enumerated. For example, if you wish to add a relative who appeared in the 1881 English census, you will be asked to supply the following information:

Piece*	**RG11/**
Folio*	(do not enter 'A' if present)
Page*	(for vessels enter '0' if missing)
Surname*	
Forename*	
Middle names or initials	
Age*	(if shown as 3/12 enter 3m or 3 months)

However, if your ancestor was in the Scottish census that same year, you would be asked to submit the following:

Volume/Registration number*	(enter as 265A, 328B-1 or 147 not 265-A, 328B/1, 328-B1 or 147/00)
Enumeration district*	(enter as 7A, 14A or 7, not as 7/1, 14/1 or 007/00)
Page*	(omit leading zeroes, thus 007 is entered as 7)
Surname*	
Forename*	
Middle names or initials	
Age*	(if shown as 3/12 enter 3m or 3 months)

The information fields marked with an asterisk are compulsory to enter, and the details must be entered as found written on the census form – if I mark an ancestor with the surname 'Paton', for example, and a cousin does it as 'Patton', this will not flag up as a match. Once the details are uploaded, click on 'Search', and if a match is found with another member, this will be flagged up. If you are a subscriber, you can initiate contact with your cousin immediately, but if not, then you will need to wait for your cousin to contact you. The identity of both cousins remains private until you have agreed to make contact, with communication initially facilitated through the platform itself.

The more relatives that are uploaded to the site by users, the better the chance of establishing a connection. The site advises that there is an element of chance in this, in that you may be lucky and find a match instantly, or you may add up to a hundred known relatives and still not find a single hit. To maximise your chances of finding shared cousins, you should add all the members recorded within each census entry, and for as many of the censuses that the site permits you to add information.

If you do not instantly make any connections, this may simply be because no cousins have as yet registered. In due course, days, months, or even years down the line, you may suddenly discover a connection, so an initial investment in time up front may yield a positive outcome at some point in the future.

ii) Curious Fox
https://curiousfox.com
Another long-standing platform, Curious Fox was first established in 2002. As with Lost Cousins, it focuses on connecting people through

a shared ancestral fact, predominantly through a shared point of geographical origin or residence, and/or by a common surname.

There are two tiers of membership, a basic free registration and a paid subscription, with the annual subscription rate at the time of writing being just £6 per year within the UK. As well as the UK and Ireland version of Curious Fox, there is a separate US version of the site, accessible at **https://curiousfox.com/us**.

The Curious Fox site has listings for virtually every town and village within the UK and Ireland, with each having a dedicated page on the platform into which users can add posts summarising their interests about an ancestor who came from that location. You can search for a location using the dialogue box on the home page, or narrow down by using the browse function to identity the country, county and then town or village from there. If upon reading through any posts found for a particular area you come across a description of a relative, or some other information of interest about the locale, the site permits contact through an internal messaging system.

Take for example the small Perthshire hamlet of Airntully, located within the Perthshire-based parish of Kinclaven. If I look for entries for this location using the search box at the top of the screen, I am told that nobody has made a post for the hamlet as yet, but that there are twenty-two posts available from members who have a connection to somewhere within a 5-mile radius of the location; I can further customise this search range between a 1-mile and 10-mile radius. If, however, I wish to search for an ancestor in a more populated area, for example Bristol, a basic search yields some 555 entries for the city.

In addition to the main entries, each search will also permit you to view 'orphan entries', these being posts for which it may no longer be possible to contact the original scribe responsible, with the original email address registered to that user no longer working (although the original writer can remedy this by updating their contact details).

An alternative way to use the site is through the 'Surname Geosearch' facility, which will permit me to search for entries for a particular surname across the UK and Ireland, or by narrowing to a county and/ or village, within a determined search radius focused on that location. A search of the name Paton, for example, yields some thirty-eight entries across the UK and Ireland at the time of writing, which I can now explore to see if any concern my family – a facility that can be particularly useful if you have a rare surname in the family.

Entries on any page are created with a header, which will be written in a red or green font, reflecting the subscription status of the poster. If a person has a free membership, then their post will have a red header, and it will not be possible to make contact with them unless you have a paid membership. If a person has a paid membership, then their header will be in green, and you will be able to contact them through the site whether you have a paid subscription or not. The bottom line is that at least one person wishing to communicate must have a paid subscription.

iii) Google My Maps
www.google.co.uk/maps/d (www.google.co.uk/mymaps)
Google's My Maps allows you to create personalised maps using a Google map as the base layer, with your own data overlaid. It can be accessed from a browser, through a dedicated Google My Maps app for mobile phones and portable devices, and even through the basic Google Maps app.

My Maps can be used for a variety of family history purposes. For example you could collaboratively work with relatives on a map to plot the migration of a particular branch of a family by tagging the various places worldwide where they have resided over a period of time, or perhaps tag the graveyards where ancestors are known to have been buried. Projects can be shared with particular individuals or groups upon invitation, or can be published for the whole world to view.

To create a map you will first need to register a Google account. Once signed in, visit the My Maps page and you will see a box that allows you to 'Create a New Map'. On clicking this you will be taken to a Google Maps screen, but you will see small white dialogue box at the top left with various menu options to help with the creation of your bespoke map. To make a start, click on 'Add layer', and give it a name, e.g. 'Birth locations'. The 'Base map' drop-down menu at the bottom of the box will then allow you to select the type of view that you can pin data points on to, such as a satellite, terrain, or simple atlas view.

On the main map screen, you will see a search box at the top, through which you can locate an area of interest, and once found, you can add a location pin or marker to it, and give a short description about it in the dialogue box to which it connects. The marker pins can be colour coded using the 'Style' box in the box, so that, for example, all births in one branch of a family can be pinned with one colour, and another colour used for births for a different ancestral line. You can also add an image, photograph or video using the camera icon in the box, which can be imported from your computer, a camera, Google Drive, Google Images, or YouTube. Once added, when you return to the main map and click on a pin with your mouse, the image or video will be displayed. On the main map you can also draw lines, or even plot routes between locations, using the on screen tools available.

You can create as many layers as you like – for example one showing birth locations, with another showing death locations. You can view each layer individually or select between layers as to which you might wish to view at any one time, by simply ticking or unticking their name in the white menu box at the top left of the page.

Using the 'Share' option in the menu box allows you to invite people to collaborate, and you can select the editing privileges that you might wish them to have. The 'Preview' button also allows you to view how the map will be viewed, and provides an option to share it publicly via Facebook, Twitter or email.

Note that when in Google Maps (**www.google.co.uk/maps**) itself, you can easily access your My Maps pages as follows. From the main menu, scroll down to the 'Your places' item. When the Your places menu pops up, click on the last option, 'Maps', and your My Maps pages will be listed. Clicking on a page name will take you to the public version of the page; click on 'Open in My Maps' if you wish to work further on the page.

iv) Historypin
www.historypin.org
Historypin is another project that uses Google Maps, allowing users to add images and videos to a base map, and within themed collections.

In addition to the basic map, a fun way to explore the history of a place is to try to overlay historic images on to Google Streetview in such a way that you can mix between the two views, then and now.

Historypin is a fun and interactive site to 'pin' historic images to a Google map, to invite discussion.

Historypin encourages users to create collections, either by adding an image with a pin to a map, or by 're-pinning' another user's previously loaded image as the starting point for a new collection. Within each collection you can leave contact details for people to get in touch with you should you wish to encourage collaboration. You can also share individual images through social media platforms.

Historypin takes a bit of practice to use, but fortunately the site has several useful videos in its Getting Started section at **https://about. historypin.org/how-to-guides**.

Cloud sharing

There are many ways to digitally store files, the most traditional method being to do so on a computer's hard drive, providing not only immediate access to records but access without a requirement for any internet provision. Balancing the pros are the cons, namely the possibility of locally held files becoming corrupted at some stage and completely unreadable, or the experience of a catastrophic computer hard-drive failure – something yours truly has personally experienced in the past and never wishes to again!

To prevent such disasters from happening, and the potential loss of years' worth of research, it is always a wise exercise to regularly back up your files on to a separate device or storage facility, such as an external hard drive, or indeed, drives, as one backup may not be enough, should it fail also.

An alternative, however, is to store a backup of your files on to an online cloud-based facility, in the same way that your emails are today stored online. If the worst truly does happen, a copy can simply be retrieved and installed as and where it is required, but in addition to this, there is the added advantage of being able to access your content from any device at any time (as long as you have internet access), and an ability to share content with others online, simply by granting them access to a cloud-based drive, a folder or a specific file.

There are far too many cloud-based programmes to discuss that can facilitate the sharing of information stored online, but to provide a flavour of the potential available, the following are some of the more common:

i) Dropbox
www.dropbox.com
Dropbox is a cloud-based storage site offering users an ability to store files and images within folders, and to keep them 'in sync' with files

hosted on another device. In addition, you can also share files with others, and collaborate on them together. In the UK, a Dropbox Basic account (**www.dropbox.com/en_GB/basic**) offers 2GB of free storage, but it is possible to pay for additional space.

I use Dropbox for a range of issues. In addition to storing a copy of my own family history research on the platform, I also use it regularly as a means to pass on research reports and accompanying documents that may be simply too large to email to clients. When giving presentations, I will use it to host accompanying document handouts, and will inform those attending of the relevant file address before I speak. This allows attendees an option up front of seeing my notes before I talk so that they can decide if they need to take additional notes throughout, or to simply sit back and listen. In addition, I also use Dropbox to host copies of my PowerPoint presentations for talks when travelling away from home as a backup, or to transfer copies of PowerPoint to others who may wish to host them for online webinars.

It is possible to save your files on your home computer within Dropbox, which will allow them to be constantly synchronised with the same files hosted on the cloud. By creating an account on Dropbox through your browser, you can download and install the programme on to your PC or Mac for free. After opening your new Dropbox folder, you can drag and drop files into its 'Documents' area. As the file is synchronising between your computer and the online Dropbox storage area, a small blue circle with two arrows will be displayed; upon completing the upload, the circle will turn green with a white tick to confirm the job is done. Anytime you access this file from now on within the Dropbox folder, any changes made to it will be automatically synchronised with the version hosted online. If you then access this folder online from another device, and make changes, these can also then be automatically synchronised back to your home computer when it is next switched on. A Dropbox app is available for installation on a mobile phone or tablet device also.

Alternatively, if you prefer to simply use your online Dropbox areas as an additional drive, you can simply add documents manually to this through a browser. From your computer drag and drop files from a folder on to the open home page of your account on the website, or use its upload functions to browse and to add a folder of interest from your device.

Sharing files and folders with others is equally easy. Within the Dropbox folder on your home computer, simply right click on the document or folder of interest, and use the option to 'Share This Folder' or 'Share Dropbox Link', which will allow you to do so by email, or to

Dropbox is a cloud storage site that allows you to share files with invited users.

paste into a document for others to read and extract at a later date. If wishing to share from your online account, simply click on the 'Share' button beside the relevant file or folder, and type in the email address of the recipient or recipients. Links can be set to expire after a set duration, and it is possible to add password protection to them and/or to set an option forbidding files to be downloaded by other users.

There are of course many alternatives to Dropbox, offering similar capabilities, including iCloud (**www.icloud.com**), Microsoft One Drive (**https://onedrive.live.com**), and Google Drive (**https://drive.google.com**).

ii) Google Docs
https://docs.google.com

Google Docs is a software package that exists within Google Drive, which allows you to create text-based documents and to export them to other devices through a variety of file types, including Microsoft Word (.docx), PDF (.pdf), OpenDocument (.odt), plain text (.rtf) and even a web page (.html). The package can be freely accessed on a home computer, also through an app on tablet and mobile phone devices (as long as you have a Google account), and it allows you to read and work on files whilst on the move.

Accompanying Google Docs is the spreadsheet-based Google Sheets, the presentations programme Google Slides, and the data collection software Google Forms, all of which equally allow you to output documents in Microsoft- and Open Data-based file formats, amongst others.

As with file sharing on Dropbox, Google Docs allows you to invite people to read or collaborate on a file using a dedicated Share button in the main menu. Documents can also be downloaded to a device. If two or more people access a file at the same time, each can view the other's changes to the text in real time.

iii) Evernote
www.evernote.com
Evernote is a cloud-based programme that allows you to store notes for various projects, not only by writing down information, but by recording audio, through images by a camera on your device, or by taking screengrabs of web pages, or parts of web pages using its 'web clipper' tool.

The information gathered can be stored as 'notes' or within 'notebooks', which can be accessed between different devices using the same account details. It is also possible to share content that has been saved with other users, to permit collaboration.

There is a basic free version, or you can upgrade to an Evernote Premium or Evernote Business option with further functionality.

Amongst Evernote's competitors is Microsoft's OneNote (**www. onenote.com**), which is now free and offers similar digital notebook functions, including the ability to share content with people you may wish to collaborate with on a project.

Crowdsourcing projects
Another way that many family historians try to contribute towards the family history world from the comfort of their own homes is to participate in what are known as 'crowdsourcing' projects. The idea behind crowdsourcing is that a project that would be seemingly insurmountable for a single person to achieve can be much more effectively tackled by a team of volunteers whether in a locally based community or around the world. Such projects can include mass efforts to transcribe large records collections, or to perhaps seek to contribute a small part of a story to a much larger picture.

A good example of a massive transcription collaboration in recent times can be seen with the release of the United States 1940 census, which was placed online for the first time in 2012. A public effort to create an index where none had previously existed surpassed all expectations – on 1 July 2012, in a single 24-hour period, the *1940 US Census Community Project,* led by FamilySearch (p.7) in partnership with the US-based National Archives and Records Administration, saw 46,000 online volunteers index more than 10.3 million records. Today the idea of regular transcription events is an increasingly common occurrence.

The recent four-year-long commemoration of the centenary of the First World War was another opportunity for several crowdsourcing efforts to get underway, where the source was the public itself. *The Lives of the First World War* project was one such initiative from the Imperial War Museum and FindmyPast, which ran from 12 May 2014 to 19 March 2019, and which encouraged the public to collaborate and bring to life the stories of many of those who participated in the conflict, to save them for posterity. The fruits of the project are now hosted by the IWM on a dedicated digital memorial platform at **https://livesofthefirstworldwar.iwm.org.uk**.

The variety of projects produced was magnificent – for the city of Glasgow alone, the following were just some of the 'Communities'-based projects that were created as part of the platform:

- Glasgow Necropolis
- Glasgow School of Arts
- The Hamiltons of Glasgow
- Anderson Brothers of Glasgow and Largo
- Alumni of the University of Glasgow
- Freemasons of Glasgow
- Queens Own regiment of Glasgow Yeomanry
- Distant Relatives & Glasgow Academy Cadets 1902
- Glasgow Celtic Football Club in the First World War
- McCulloch Brothers
- Quintinshill Rail Disaster
- The Sellier Brothers from Trinidad, West Indies
- The Lodge of Glasgow St John No. 3bis
- Lodge St Vincent Sandyford No. 553
- HMS *Perugia* (Q-1): 3 December 1916

Another of the conflict-themed collaborations was a series of roadshows carried out across Europe by the Europeana project, in which people were invited to bring along First World War memorabilia to be seen by experts and digitised for posterity. Between 2012 and 2014 the roadshow visited Boston Spa in Yorkshire, Banbury, Preston and Dublin, as well as venues in Germany, Luxembourg, Slovenia and Denmark to gather materials. Members of the public were invited to come along and to have historic items in their possession associated with the conflict scanned for posterity, along with any relevant stories. The material gathered is now included at **www.europeana.eu**.

Crowdsourcing is an effective and fun means to help empower the wider genealogical community with the resources it needs to pursue research further, with several online platforms offering regular opportunities to participate. The following are some of the key projects available if you fancy having a go yourself:

i) World Archives Project

Ancestry's dedicated records indexing project is accessible under the Help menu option at the top of the home screen, and then by selecting 'Community'. A piece of software called a 'Keying Tool' needs to be downloaded to allow you to participate, available at **www. familytreemaker.com/AWAP/** for both PC and Mac computers.

The project offers a variety of ongoing datasets to work on at any one time, and there are some perks for participation as a transcriber, such as free and early access to the entire collection worked upon prior to any release to the public, as well as discounts on subscriptions for more active contributors. Ancestry also donates copies of record indexes and images from the project to partnering archives and family history societies. When a dataset is complete, the indexes are made freely available to access on the Ancestry site, although to view the original records you will require a subscription.

Having downloaded and installed the Keying Tool, and opened it from your desktop, you will need to sign in with an Ancestry account, although a basic free account is enough to gain access without the need

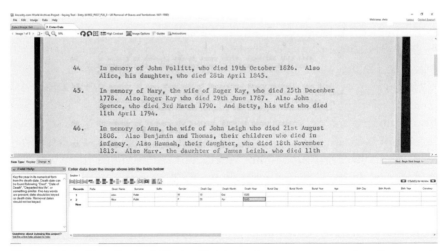

The World Archives Project's Keying Tool is a software programme that allows you to create a searchable crowdsourced archive database in collaboration with hundreds of other volunteers.

to obtain a subscription. You can then obtain record sets to work on from the button at the top right corner of the home page marked 'Download Image Sets'. A pop-up screen will list the sets available, from which you can make your selection and download the relevant image set to work on. Having done so, open the collection that has been downloaded and a separate transcription screen will emerge, with the document image in the top half and the transcriber tool to the bottom. A separate pop-up screen will also arrive entitled 'Project Instruction' outlining what needs to be transcribed. Having read this and closed it, a series of 'Help Getting Started' tips will emerge to steer you through what you need to do. If you disable these at any stage you can turn them back on again by clicking the 'Turn on "Help Getting Started" Tips' item under the Help menu.

The site takes a little getting used to, but a dedicated help section with tips and videos can be access on the project's wiki via **https:// wiki.rootsweb.com//wiki/index.php?title=Ancestry_World_Archives_ Project**.

The site offers a blog at **https://blogs.ancestry.com/worldarchivesproject** providing progress reports on current and forthcoming projects, and there are social media platforms available on Facebook at **www.facebook.com/ AncestryWorldArchivesProject** and Twitter at **@WorldArchives**.

ii) FamilySearch Indexing

Also operating on a worldwide basis is the volunteer-based FamilySearch Indexing project. FamilySearch (p.7) has literally millions of holdings in its archive in Utah, which for many years have existed on microfilm but which are now being digitised. The indexing project is the means to help unlock the many secrets held within the records. Unlike Ancestry's offering, the tools required for indexing record sets are now available on the FamilySearch platform itself, accessible as a main menu item on the home page. You will require a FamilySearch account, but no software needs to be downloaded to your home computer.

The indexing menu has four sub-headings – 'Overview', 'Web Indexing', 'Find a Project' and 'Indexing Help'. The first provides an Overview, where you can take a tour of the platform's indexing tool and actually practise transcribing entries on a project through a series of steps, but without needing to save the results. If you get a transcribed field wrong during this training session, the site will point out what should have been recorded, allowing you to develop the confidence to continue.

When you feel ready to get stuck in properly, the Web Indexing menu tab takes you to a page where you can select new projects to work on and where you can monitor the progress of those that you have already chosen. By clicking on 'Find a Batch' you can locate new projects by name, language and difficulty level (Beginning, Intermediate, or Advanced). You can also identify further challenges through the Find a Project menu option, which hosts an interactive map depicting which continents have active projects available to work on. Through this you can browse the offerings per country, with each listed alongside a graphic indicating how much of that dataset has already been indexed, and how much of that work has been reviewed by the FamilySearch team to check for accuracy. If a project is of particular interest, you can click on 'Start Indexing Now' to get stuck in.

After a batch is loaded, a pop-up window with 'Project Instructions' will immediately appear, offering basic information on the job to hand, indicating the types of entries to be recorded, as well as how to address information that is not available or not required. Examples of documents that have already been transcribed are provided, which are worth exploring before you start, and various tips will also be offered. Once you close the Project Instructions window, you can always reopen it for further guidance at any stage as you work, via a link to the left-hand side of the page.

It may all seem a bit overwhelming to start with, but you will soon get into the routine of indexing in the required manner for that particular dataset. The top of the project screen has a variety of menu options with

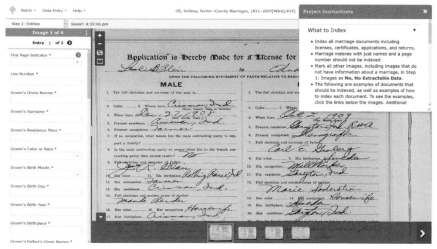

The FamilySearch Indexing tool is located on the website itself, with full instructions available for how to record data from each image in a collection.

additional help resources. The 'Data Entry' menu, for example, offers a ruler that you can use to highlight a line as you work on it, which can be particularly helpful when working on a document with handwriting, as well as a facility to view 'reference images', if you are unclear about what a particular image is trying to convey before you. The 'Help' menu also has many useful tools, including a handy 'Basic indexing guidelines' page.

At the top right of the page is another handy facility, a small box marked 'Tips', which, amongst its offerings, provides a link to 'Ask a Question in the Indexing Community', where you can seek particular guidance on a dataset from more experienced indexers, as well as being able meet and get to know many fellow participants!

iii) FreeUKGEN
www.freeukgenealogy.org.uk
First established in 1998, FreeUKGEN is one of the world's longest-running crowdsourcing projects, with a well-deserved reputation for quality control. As a Charitable Incorporated Organisation it currently oversees three separate volunteer-based open data projects designed to help genealogists specifically within Britain.

FreeBMD (**www.freebmd.org.uk**) is perhaps the best known, and is a volunteer project designed to create a free-to-access index to the records of births, marriages and deaths in England and Wales from 1837–1983, as compiled through the civil registration process. Its sister project FreeCen (**www.freecen.org.uk**) has a similarly long standing mission to provide free-to-access transcriptions of the decennial censuses in Scotland, England and Wales from 1841–1891, whilst FreeReg (**www.freereg.org. uk**) focuses specifically on church records of births/baptisms, marriages and burials/deaths, including both state parish churches and the records of nonconformist denominations.

Whichever project you may wish to participate in, you will be given full training before you start. If we take FreeReg as an example, from the 'Volunteer' menu option at **www.freeukgenealogy.org.uk**, navigate to the 'Transcriber Opportunities' page and then click on 'FreeReg'. This will take you through to the project's 'Transcriber Registration' page, which explains the basic set up of the project, where you will be invited to choose from one of the groups of volunteers (known as syndicates) that is currently requiring assistance. As part of the registration process you will be asked to read and agree to several documents, including the 'Transcription Agreement', the 'Volunteer Induction' handbook, the 'Code of Conduct' and the 'Volunteer Policy'. Upon successful registration you will receive log-in details to help you access the project's transcription system.

Once registered you will be provided with a point of contact called a Syndicate Coordinator, with whom you can communicate to discuss issues, and who will monitor your progress and act as a friendly mentor. A County Coordinator will also be available (who may well be the same person as the Syndicate Coordinator), who oversees what work is available for that county, and with whom you will need to correspond for additional opportunities when your chosen assignments are complete.

The basic set up is that FreeReg will allow you to download an image to your computer and request that you transcribe its contents, before uploading the file back to the server. If you have a Windows-based computer, the project offers a transcription programme called WinREG, but will also take a spreadsheet from an office-based software programme; if your computer is instead a Mac- or Linux-based system, then spreadsheets are the only available option.

A page at **www.freereg.org.uk/cms/information-for-transcribers** provides all the basic information needed for transcribers, including how to communicate with team members. In addition to this there is also a dedicated Facebook group for members to share their experiences and wisdom, and project volunteers will also receive a regular newsletter.

iv) UKIndexer

https://ukindexer.co.uk

TheGenealogist platform offers a money saving incentive to volunteers through its UK Indexer project. By indexing records such as headstone-based monumental inscriptions and census records, or by photographing headstones and submitting them to the platform, you can earn credits in return for use on TheGenealogist platform or its sister site at **www. GenealogySupplies.com**.

To subscribe to the project, you first need to register through the main UKIndexer website. A list of available projects is available from the home page, and once you have selected one to work you will be asked to read the introduction to the collection, and to note the details about the transcription effort, including the difficulty notes and the number of credits you will be rewarded upon completion. A list of instructions then appears and once you have read these you can then volunteer for a batch to work on by clicking the green button to the top of the page. After clarifying what kind of image you will be working on (e.g. from a page or a headstone), you will then be given a data entry panel to work on, to input the relevant information found. A video tutorial at **https://**

youtu.be/KsOuneAVT4o will guide you through how to successfully transcribe and submit your end results.

One thing to be aware of is that if you download a batch to work on, you will need to complete it within seven days; you can return it back to the site if for any reason you are unable to complete it. Once you have finished a batch you can select another and then continue.

v) FindaGrave
www.findagrave.com
At the time of writing FindaGrave styles itself as the 'world's largest gravesite collection' with over 180 million transcribed memorials created worldwide by its members since 1995. It offers various tools for the newcomer, including a virtual tour of the platform and a series of video tutorials to guide on the basics, both in contributing to the site and in using it.

Participants can add photos of gravestones to online-based 'virtual cemeteries', as well as transcribed monumental inscriptions, memorials, biographies, and even photos of the deceased, either through a desktop computer at home or out and about at a cemetery itself, using a dedicated app on a smart phone or tablet. Using an Apple device or an Android-based phone you can add GPS (Global Positioning Data) data to the information you are adding, which will help visitors to the cemetery to locate where the headstone photographed may be found. This can be done by selecting Location Services in your phone's Settings option, and the GPS coordinates will be uploaded with any image you take. GPS coordinates can also be added manually to any image already available on the site.

If you wish to become more active, the platform also offers templates for spreadsheets through which you can collate the data for many memorials and submit in one batch. Users can also suggest edits on other people's submissions.

The site itself is free to search, and users can leave a virtual flower on a page. Those who create entries or leave virtual flowers can in turn be contacted as a further means to facilitate connections with potential relatives.

vi) BillionGraves.com
www.billiongraves.com
Billion Graves has a similar mission to FindaGrave, styling itself as the 'world's largest resource for searchable GPS cemetery data'.

As with FindaGrave, Billion Graves allows volunteers to upload photos of headstones from around the world to virtual cemeteries, either through a PC or through a dedicated smartphone app, and to enable GPS coordinates data to be uploaded alongside transcriptions of the content.

Through partnership arrangements with some of the key genealogy records vendors it also permits record searches. The site also offers various help resources including training videos for those wishing to carry out such work for the first time.

vii) Online Parish Clerks

Several counties in England have volunteer-based website projects dedicated to providing free genealogical access to records concerning their particular patch, known as Online Parish Clerks (OPC). Details of current OPC projects can be found at **www.familysearch.org/wiki/en/Online_Parish_Clerks** and at **www.ukbmd.org.uk/online_parish_clerk**.

The longest established OPC project is that for Cornwall at **www.opc-cornwall.org**, which has volunteers based around the world transcribing records and offering free assistance to those making enquiries. These records go beyond the basic vital records of births, marriages and deaths, and can include records as diverse as apprenticeship indentures, court records, bastardy cases and school admissions.

The various OPCs can be contacted through their websites should you wish to consider offering your services as a volunteer, or if you require assistance.

viii) GENUKI

www.genuki.org.uk

First established in 1995, GENUKI is a free-to-access online reference library for genealogical resources and advice for the UK and Ireland, as well as the Isle of Man and the Channel Islands. Through the site, individual volunteers adopt a particular county, town or parish, and provide information about primary resources that may assist for research within that area (including some transcriptions), as well as information about research establishments, societies and just about anything else that might assist.

Due to the volunteer nature of the site, some pages are more detailed than others, and enquiries about participation are encouraged by contacting the site's volunteer coordinator.

Wiki projects

'Wiki' platforms are HTML-based websites (p.117), which are written collaboratively by users to produce articles which can be updated by others through an ongoing process of collaboration. The most famous

The FIBIS Fibiwiki site is a wiki-based collaborative encyclopaedia compiled by the society's volunteers to provide resources to help trace British Indian ancestry.

wiki site by far is the Wikimedia Foundation's Wikipedia platform at **www.wikipedia.org**, a giant of an encyclopaedia to which anyone can make a contribution, with over 6 million articles written in English alone.

There are many wiki platforms within the genealogy world also, the most famous of which is perhaps the FamilySearch Research Wiki at **www.familysearch.org/wiki**, with over 90,000 articles at the time of writing. The platform encourages contributions, and offers various Help articles to get you on your way.

The Families in British India Society (p.10) has another well-known wiki platform – its FibiWiki site at **https://wiki.fibis.org** – for users to share information about researching ancestors in India. The site contains guides, source lists and background information on a variety of topics. If you wish to contribute, either by supplying content or editing material already available, you simply contact the society's webmaster and request for an account to be set up in your name.

The International Society of Genetic Genealogy wiki at **https://isogg. org/wiki** is another powerful platform for advice on the use of DNA for family history (see Chapter 5). To contribute you need to join ISOGG and similarly register for an account.

For a useful digest of available genealogy-themed wikis, visit Cyndi's List at **www.cyndislist.com/wikis**.

Chapter 4

RECORDING YOUR FAMILY HISTORY

There are many ways that we can record our family history, as well as to store the various documents and other sources which we use to create our ancestral stories. For many people nothing will ever beat using a quill and parchment, or a pen and paper, but increasingly popular today are family tree programmes, available both online and offline. Not only do such platforms allow us to input the data from our ancestral research, they also provide us with a handy one-stop-shop for data management, as well as a bespoke tool from which we can further generate charts and reports on key branches or individuals within our ancestry.

Sharing a tree online brings many additional benefits to the party. In addition to it providing a means for others to see your work, it can also act as a further data backup, should something catastrophic happen in the home environment leading to the loss of all the research gathered to date. Used creatively, an online-hosted tree can actually work as a tool to help generate new leads for research.

On the flip side, placing a family tree online requires responsibility to protect the privacy of the living (p.14), and whilst many free programmes exist online, their true potential may not be unlocked without a regular subscription payment towards the host. Furthermore, if your research is only hosted online, you are completely at the mercy of the fortunes of the company hosting your material, and you will certainly need to make sure that you are happy with its terms and conditions (p.17), and can keep on top of any changes that may be made to these in due course.

In this chapter I will look at some of the many platforms available, but in particular, show how they can be used to make our research work for us and help us expand the ancestral stories that we wish to tell in the first place.

Software packages

Many superb family tree software packages can be purchased for use on your PC or Mac, which do not require you to go online in order to create a family tree or to record your ancestry. The following are some of the better known offerings:

Family Historian	**www.family-historian.co.uk**
Family Tree Maker	**www.mackiev.com/ftm**
Legacy	**https://legacyfamilytree.com**
Heredis	**www.heredis.com/en**
Reunion	**www.leisterpro.com**
Roots Magic	**www.rootsmagic.co.uk**
TreeView	**https://treeview.co.uk**

At their most basic, such programmes can allow you to create individual entries for each known relative within your ancestry, with options to document the sources found from which your understanding of such individuals emerges. You can also easily manipulate the information in different ways once it has been input into your programme, for example, with a click of a button, a family group sheet (noting all the individuals within a particular branch of your tree) can be converted into a family tree diagram. Each programme also has its own loyal community of users, who can collaborate through social media and forums to discuss issues, ranging from genealogical advice to technical problems.

Some packages may be simply stand-alone offerings which will only host information about your family, but in an increasingly interactive world many programmes will also engage with online resources, for example to search particular websites and data platforms to try to find records with which you can populate your tree, and to draw down such information to your computer for storage. Digitally created family tree programmes can offer so much more, however, if you allow the information on your family itself to be shared with other family members.

No matter which software you use, there will almost certainly be a facility to export the file you create, which you can email to someone you may be collaborating with. Many programmes will have their own file standards, but one of the greatest-ever achievements within the history of digital genealogy was the creation of a file standard called GEDCOM (which stands for GEnealogical Data COMmunications) by the Church of Jesus Christ of Latter-day Saints, which is almost universally recognised throughout the genealogical world. A GEDCOM file is easily recognised as one that ends with '.ged' at the end, and which can be opened by most, if not all, family history software programmes, whether offline or online. Whilst such files are best used in a family tree programme, the files can be opened with a text-based document also, from which information can also be extracted.

A key thing to remember about any data stored on your home computer is that if the device fails at any stage, you may very well end up losing everything you have worked on for years. As such, it is crucial that you back up your research regularly on external drives, so that if your PC or Mac heads for the great digital afterlife at any stage, you can immediately restore your data to another device and pick up from where you left off. There are many places in which such backups can be stored, but one alternative way to avoid disaster is to host your tree online, either as data stored in a cloud-based storage platform (p.55), or through a platform offering an online family tree provision.

Online programmes

Many of the main genealogy vendor platforms host family tree capabilities, not only to allow users to try to find matches from within their vast data collections but also to try to find connections with distant cousins and relatives who may well be researching the same individuals. On viewing a shared tree online, a brick wall that you may have been struggling with for some time might well have been overcome already by a cousin, and a problem shared can certainly be a problem halved. You may also find from a cousin's tree that you may have missed something, or that you have been unaware of an entirely different story, perhaps a second marriage of an ancestor beyond your direct line.

My online-hosted tree is a visual projection of my ancestral history, but it is also my family history essentially 'weaponised' as a means to locate additional information through collaboration. I have made many wonderful connections as a result, not least when also used in collaboration with the testing of my DNA (Chapter 5), and I have located many forgotten resources held by distant cousins, such as old family photographs, unknown stories, and considerably more as a consequence.

However, a word of caution! Whilst you and I may well be the wisest, kindliest, most diligent family historians ever bequeathed unto mankind, the distant cousins suggested from discoveries within online-hosted family trees may not be, if indeed they are our distant cousins in the first place. With every advantage from an online tree comes a disadvantage. One of the greatest is the ability for people to see what you have placed online, to appropriate it for their own use, and to then royally screw it up further with their own horrendous efforts.

Somebody may well come along, see your John Smith, put two and two together to come up with a spectacular five, and then claim your ancestor as their own, with absolutely no justification for having done so, other than 'they thought it was him' or that 'he had the same name, and was in the same place, so it must be him'. There are some folk out there who simply want to have a large family tree that will look good when printed out, and others may genuinely try to put square pegs into round holes, to try to justify a claim their granny once told them about relating to their alleged descent from Charlemagne, William the Conqueror, Robert the Bruce, or Niall of the Nine Hostages. On such trees you may find a purported cousin dying or being baptised before they were born, marrying their mother and then their grandmother, and also being the Queen's forgotten cousin, step-sister or child. Their profile picture may carry a 'family coat of arms' to reflect their quickly found nobility, possibly replicated with a full matching merchandise range with which they have then decorated their luxurious apartments.

Believe me, mistakes on online trees happen *a lot*. Be prepared for the fact that if you put your research online, it will be taken and added to the trees of others, and in some cases then added to with some quite astonishing errors. Once such errors happen, they are soon replicated by others also trying to grow their tree in a day, and before you know it, the truth of your ancestral story may be soon swamped by nonsense that you were not responsible for creating in the first place. Just for good measure, both you and your tree may then be cited as the source and evidence for such mangled disasters.

A lot of people get very upset when they see such mistakes appear on other trees. You might wish to contact them to point out such errors, and on occasion you may get a cordial response acknowledging the problem, and offering to work with you to examine where an error may have been made. When this happens, it is a joy, but do also be prepared for the fact that other responses are potentially available.

I tend to be quite bluntly philosophical about my online tree. I am more than happy for people to look at what I have, to interrogate it, to argue with it, to utilise my finds for their trees if it will help, and also to flag up errors if I make them, which I will respond to positively, with an evidence-based approach. Not everybody is of the same mindset, and not everybody has the same end goal in mind – but that really is for them to deal with. I am not the guardian of the genealogical universe, my actual responsibility when creating an online tree is simply to my children and family, for whom I am carrying out such research in the first place. Whilst many years ago I may have been upset to see my work appropriated in dubious ways by others, I have also benefited from those who have positively embellished my work through their friendly and professional collaboration.

The following are some of the more popular offerings available online:

i) Ancestry
www.ancestry.co.uk

Ancestry is a massive name within the family history world as a provider of online digital records from around the world, but one of its most useful features is its tree-building programme. This is free to use even if you have not subscribed to access any of the site's digital records, you simply need to sign up for a free basic account.

You can upload a GEDCOM family tree file from a programme on your home computer to create such a tree, or build one from scratch, and it is possible to make the tree accessible to the public or to keep it private. In addition, you can also grant other people permission to work on your tree, permitting a wonderful means for online collaboration.

Ancestry's family tree programme is also compatible with the most recent Family Tree Maker (**www.mackiev.com**) software package for a home computer, with which you can work offline and then synchronise with your online tree when back online. In a similar light, Ancestry has a freely available dedicated app for mobile devices and tablets, through which you can also work on your tree.

When you start building your tree on Ancestry, you are offered a chance to add yourself as a home person, with details of first and middle

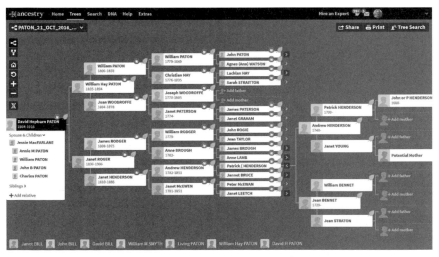

Ancestry's operation not only permits users to build an online searchable family tree, it can also be used to locate genetic cousins if the user has taken a DNA test.

names, surname, a suffix, gender, birth date and birthplace. If you choose to name somebody else as a home person, then further fields for a death date and death place are also made available. Upon saving the details you are returned to the tree view, and asked to add a spouse, and/or parental details, at which point you are then asked to name your tree, and whether you would like others to view it (with those marked as 'living' hidden for privacy purposes). Upon clicking 'Save tree', you now have a family tree file available online which can be searched for by others if you have kept it public.

Once saved, the default view now changes to a vertically based pedigree view with a few more bells and whistles. To the left, a menu allows you to switch between vertical and horizontal tree views, with a control to allow you to zoom in or widen out. You can also click on an icon to take you to the home person; a further function allows you to synchronise your tree with one on your home computer. On this view, the boxes providing information about individuals are very basic, depicting just a person's name, a photograph of that person if one has been added (or a silhouette image of a man or a woman, based on the sex of the person), and years of birth and death. If there is an image of a leaf in the top right of the box, this will denote the number of 'Ancestry Hints' available for that person, flagging up potential appearances of that individual within other people's trees, or records which may be relevant, all of which you can review or ignore. If you have your DNA test results connected to your tree, potential ThruLines matches will be suggested in the top left of the box, via a blue circular graphic depicting a small family (see p.99).

If upon reviewing these hints you agree that they are relevant, you can look at the suggestions for links on other people's trees (if they are set to public access), and also import any relevant records into your tree. The records you can see, however, will very much depend on the type of subscription that you have. If, for example, you have a UK-based subscription, and have an ancestor who was born in England, you may find relevant records from there as part of your package – but if he or she later moved to the USA, and is then flagged up as having been in the 1930 and 1940 censuses there, those images will not be available to view unless you upgrade your account to permit access to the American records. You can also hang fire for a bit if you are undecided about confirming a link, or completely ignore the suggestions made altogether. One other key thing to be aware of is that if you do create a link to any records found hosted on Ancestry, these can only be viewed subsequently if you continue to have an active paid subscription.

At the top right, a separate menu allows you to share your tree with other potential collaborators, to allow others 'the right to view, contribute to, or edit your tree'. You can email a person to invite them to participate, or search for them by their Ancestry user name. You can also create a shareable link which you can directly email to a person, to provide access to your tree with particular restrictions, by allowing a person the role of guest, contributor or editor, and the right to see living people or not. In addition, this menu also allows you a facility to print your tree, or to look for particular individuals through the 'Tree Search' option, which then makes the person searched for the centre of proceedings if successfully located and his or her name clicked upon.

One of the more fun and useful aspects of Ancestry's package is the ability to contribute additional information to a person's profile. Clicking on the name of an individual in the tree brings up a mini menu with four options. The third and fourth options allow you to perform a quick edit on your relative's box on the tree, or to view their tree, to add a relative, a tag, or to delete that person. If you click on the second option, 'Search', you can look through Ancestry's extensive collection of records and family trees, but again, although matches may be flagged up, you can only view the record if you have a relevant paid subscription.

Clicking on the first option, 'Profile', brings you into the real work area of the site. The Profile view allows you to add and see a chronological view of facts and events within that person's lifetime, the names of his or her parents, spouse and any children. In addition to this you can add notes about a person, comments, and tags, for example flagging up if they are a DNA match (see p.97), the status of your research into them, or the confidence of any conclusions you have reached concerning the validity of their relationship to you.

Another essential section is that for 'Sources', in which you can search for records on Ancestry, document the locations of other records and/ or web links that have been found and contributed to that individual's narrative. Ancestry's source citations are generally quite good, and you can use their form of source citation, or create your own.

There are many other nifty tips and tricks available on Ancestry's platform. The 'LifeStory' tab allows you to view a chronology of an individual in which you can add 'historical insights', facts that can add historical context to the period within that individual is found to have existed. There is also a 'Gallery' area into which you can add photos and a 'Story' facility. The Story function allows you to write a story directly into that person's profile, or to upload one already written on your computer, and you can very handily append this to the profile of more than one individual. In addition to posting what you do know about an individual, this is also as good an area as any to ask questions about what you do not know – a further line of bait to encourage a response from anybody reading who might just have the answers. There is also a further link to the Ancestry Hints area.

Ancestry's family tree platform is one of the very best that is available online, and is particularly useful – in fact essential – to utilise should you wish to carry out any DNA research on the platform to confirm connections with distant cousins. This will be discussed further in Chapter 5.

ii) MyHeritage
www.myheritage.com

MyHeritage's online Family Tree Builder programme can be accessed for free with a Basic MyHeritage subscription, but with a tree size limit of 250 individuals, and an online storage limit of 500 MB for media items, with both of these limits lifted upon signing up for a paid subscription. The programme can be downloaded to a home computer via **www. myheritage.com/family-tree-builder**, and changes can be synchronised with the online-hosted edition at a time of your convenience. There is also an app available which permits working on the tree via mobile and tablet devices, which can also be synchronised to an online version and to that on a home computer.

The 'Family tree' tab on the main menu at the top of the MyHeritage site is where you will find the tree-building programme online. The site

MyHeritage's family tree builder.

allows you to import a GEDCOM file, or to build a tree from scratch, with yourself as the first candidate. Most of the sub-menu options provide for different functions to manage and maintain your tree, although some facilities, such as the Colorize photos tool (p.32), are really not core to the process, despite being immense fun!

The 'My family tree' view is the basic work screen. Details for an individual are shown within a basic box, coloured blue for males and pink for females, which display the person's name, years of birth and death, and an image should you wish to add one. You are also shown ghosted areas on the screen, boxes with dotted lines around them, to show where you can add the names of parents to that individual. Any other relationships already confirmed to an individual are presented in a vertically based 'Family view' diagram as a default. It is possible to change this view through a drop-down menu at the top right of the page, where you can set the page to a horizontally based 'Pedigree view', a vertically shaped 'Fan view', or a 'List view' of all candidates within the tree.

If you click on a person's dialogue box, you now get access to additional functions that will allow you to add further information. By clicking on 'Search this person' you can look for records for them in MyHeritage's database, but this is perhaps best left until a few other details have first been added. A large cross image in the middle of the menu allows you to upload a photo or even a video of the person being described, whilst beneath are a series of tools. A plus symbol when clicked on allows you to add names to a wide circle of relationships around that person (father, mother, brother, sister, partner, son or daughter), a pencil symbol when selected takes you to a profile page to fill in basic vital records facts, and a box marked 'More' allows you to view connections and relationships, and to delete the individual's entry.

The 'View full profile' link takes you to a dedicated page about that person, where you can add additional information. The 'Info' box in particular is one of the most versatile dialogue screens online in a family tree programme, allowing you to add details about a person's education, work, personal information, contact information, source citations, biographical entries, links to web-based content, and even a memories area at the very bottom, within which you can record personal anecdotes about that individual. The 'Events' page link allows you to see events in a fairly basic chronological list, although an interesting addition is a box leading to a Google maps interface showing a trail, with locations tagged at which events were stated to have occurred. The 'DNA' tab on the menu allows you to connect the tree to DNA results, including the DNA of the person featured, if that person grants you permission to do so.

There are some additional features listed under the Family tree menu at the top of the page which are unique (at the time of writing!), and which can help with the presentation of the tree. The 'Consistency checker' is a tool that scans the tree for what it considers to be obvious mistakes, such as somebody found to have died before they were born, as well as issues to do with how information may have been entered. A 'Relationship report' tool allows you to visually see the relationship between two identified individuals within a tree, whilst the 'Sources' page permits you to manage the various sources and citations of those for events documented in the tree.

MyHeritage's family tree charts are a powerful tool when combined with the company's own DNA-testing platform, helping to determine relationships on the documentary trail alongside the genetic evidence shared within the blood – this will be discussed further on p.100.

As with other platforms, MyHeritage will also use your tree to seek potential records that it holds which may be relevant for a particular individual, but will also try to establish connections with other users of its site. It does so through the following tools:

- **SuperSearch** – MyHeritage's global search system for its records also includes searches within its family trees collection
- **Record Matches** – this tool looks for family tree matches in newspaper articles, books and other free text documents
- **Instant Discoveries** – this seeks to find matches in other users trees, and to create 'packages' of content that may be missing from your own tree. The tool looks for matches for specific individuals or photos found in other family trees on MyHeritage and using record matching technologies in other family tree collections such as those on FamilySearch, with incorrect matches filtered out automatically. For this to work, trees must have fewer than 25,000 individuals included.
- **Smart Matching** – this tool searches family trees directly for common points. According to MyHeritage, the tool 'bridges across differences in spelling, phonetics, and relationships that may exist between the trees to offer a large quantity of highly accurate matches'.

It is entirely up to you whether you wish to adopt the finds made by the company and to integrate them into your tree. Further information on how these matching technologies work is available in the site's Help Centre at **https://faq.myheritage.com/en/discoveries-research**.

Note also that you can invite someone to collaborate on your family tree, which will allow them to add content such as photos, videos, documents, news articles and comments. If you edit your family tree online, members will also be able to edit your tree and invite other people to join your site. To invite people to collaborate, contact them by email via the 'Invite family' option of the 'Home' tab at the top of the home page.

iii) FindmyPast
www.findmypast.co.uk
FindmyPast's Family Tree tool is available on the home page via the first menu option at the top of the page. You do not need a paid subscription to register to create a tree, but the absence of one will inhibit the ability to use your tree to locate records from the main platform itself. A handy user guide for the programme is available at **www.findmypast.co.uk/blog/family-tree**.

FindmyPast's programme, in common with its competitors, allows you to create a tree or to import a file as a GEDCOM. If building a tree from scratch, the primary individual requires a name and a date of birth as a minimum data entry requirement. A step-through guide will allow you to then build up the initial relationships with parents and grandparents to form the basic tree.

For each individual you can select one of four views to work within:

- a vertical 'Family View' chart
- a horizontal 'Pedigree' chart
- a 'Family Group' page – showing a basic chart for an individual, spouse, parents and children
- a 'Profile' page for a specific individual.

Within either of the tree viewing modes, clicking on an individual produces a mini-menu which allows you to access their profile page, to edit their basic vital records details, to add a relative or to search for further information about them in FindmyPast's extensive collection of records. A small icon in the top right marked 'View Stories' also allows you to look for possible matching stories in FindmyPast's newspaper collection (the British Newspaper Archive, produced in collaboration with the British Library). Within the 'Media' and 'Notes' sections on an individual Profile page, photos, documents and stories about the individual can also be stored.

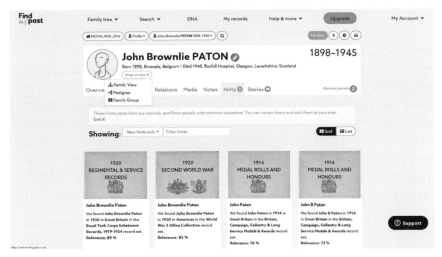

FindmyPast's tree-building programme identifies potentially matching records on the platform. In this example, the author discovered records of his great-uncle, who was found to have served with the Royal Tank Corps.

FindmyPast will handily search its site automatically for potential records that might help with your research, through a series of 'hints', which you can review, accept or reject. A small orange circle with a number inside will display the number of possible matches as hints; if a match is found, you can add it to their profile on your tree, and continue to access it if you have an active subscription. Some of the matches may not be that spectacular (especially if your ancestor is a John Smith!), and many will be vital records matches, but occasionally some absolute gems will emerge.

It was through my FindmyPast's hosted tree, for example, that a hint was flagged up for my great-uncle John Brownlie Paton as having enlisted in May 1920 with the Royal Tank Corps, not long after his release from the Ruhleben Prisoner of War camp for British civilians in 1918 (p.33). The record was a hugely important find, not just in providing evidence of an address in Scotland for my great-grandmother following her return from Belgium after the war but in noting that his own service was brief, for just a year, and further revealing that he had later re-enlisted with the Royal Army Service Corps in 1925. Without importing my tree to FindmyPast, I would simply never have known about John's stints of post-war military service, brief as they were.

If you wish for someone else to view your tree, you can email them the URL (p.116) for your tree page, which they will be able to view if they have an active account themselves. FindmyPast also advises that a tree can be made entirely private by changing the privacy setting – simply go to the 'Tree settings' icon at the top right of the Family Tree page (it looks like a small wheel).

FindmyPast has a feature called 'Tree to Tree hinting'. Through additional suggested hints, the company alerts other tree users who may have matches with some of your relatives about potential information that might assist with their own research. To enable this facility you need to tick a box marked as 'Share deceased ancestors' in the 'Tree Settings' menu, found via a small circular wheel icon link at the top right of the Family Tree page. Information on living relatives is not shared. A messaging service permits users to contact those who have tree to tree hints.

iv) TreeView
www.treeview.co.uk
A specially designed family history software programme for the United Kingdom market, TreeView was initially launched online as part of TheGenealogist website at **www.genealogist.co.uk**, before gaining its own dedicated platform in 2016. The programme is also now available on CD for installation on a home computer, further allowing users to work offline without the need to be logged into a TreeView account. Importantly, once a user decides to go back online, a simple click of a button allows the changes implemented offline to be synchronised between the home computer and the web-hosted equivalent tree on TreeView or The Genealogist. You can also synchronise the tree with a version held on an Apple or Android-based tablet and phone device, thanks to a free dedicated app available from Google Play or Apple's App store.

Once installed on to your computer, you can create a brand new family tree from scratch, load in an existing tree from another programme by uploading it as a GEDCOM file (p.69), or import an existing tree file from the TreeView website. Adding individuals, or editing details for existing members, is done through a series of interactive screens presented under the TreeView tab at the top of the screen.

Amongst the most useful options are a 'Pedigree' chart view (displaying ancestors from left to right), a 'Family' view (listing details of two parents and any children), and an 'Hourglass' view (with an individual's ancestors displayed above and descendants below), with other useful presentations including ancestral-, descendant-, fan- and circle-based trees. Should you wish to see your true place in the grand scheme of things, a Full tree is also available, depicting every branch of the tree related to the primary individual selected. It is possible to zoom in or out from the screen, and once zoomed in, to move the image by clicking on it and dragging it in the direction you wish to go. In Pedigree view you can also change the number of generations available to see at one time, from two to ten, although four to five tends to be a more manageable number.

To change the details for any individual in these charts, you simply double click on his or her name and a dialogue screen will open up, allowing basic information to be added or edited, and additional facts to be added or removed using menu options at the bottom half of the box. Facts available include the basic vital events of birth, marriage and death, as well as dozens of other options, varying from the dates of bar mitzvahs, censuses, and naturalisation, to retirement, probate and burial. As well as source citations for all information input, it is also possible to add photographs and document images for a more complete research chest. These can be carried over to your online trees when synchronising.

There are several ways to have fun with the tree data once it has been input. Various customised family charts can be created and saved through the 'Charts' dialogue box, to which the user's own background images can be added. A handy feature is that saved charts will be updated if the main file has been changed after those charts were created, as well as options to customise the colours and fonts used. Similarly, a range of genealogy reports can also be created from the top menu, detailing a person's ancestry, family view or descendants.

There are some extra fun bells and whistles with the platform. In the 'Maps' section, it is possible to locate where your ancestors' events took place, by clicking on the bottom left and viewing a corresponding marker on the map beside it. You can move this marker to exactly pinpoint the correct location. Elsewhere, under the main menu at the top of the screen you can select Find, and type in search terms such as 'soldier' or 'Perth' to produce a list of all people in your database with such words included in their descriptions.

When visiting the TreeView website for the first time, you can sign up to a 30-day trial for the full package, after which your account will default to a 'TreeView Lite' version, freely accessible but with many of the features disabled, including an ability to print. Full restoration is only possible by purchasing one of the software packages, which you can install on your computer, an advantage of this being that you can work offline on your work station and synchronise with your online-hosted tree whenever convenient. Other features are also included with the software packages, for example a four-month Diamond Subscription to TheGenealogist website, which the software will allow you to search to look for matches for records concerning individuals in your tree.

Collaborative family trees

There are many online-hosted projects which aim to create a single family tree, on which the public can work together and share information, rather than hosting individual trees which may at points overlap but which might also in parts conflict. In essence, it is a crowdsourced project into which individuals can add particular pieces of information that they hold, which may not be known to other participants, and work together as an extended research community. The idea is to save a great deal of duplicated effort, and at the same time to increase the scrutiny and accuracy on reported relationships.

One thing to be aware of with collaborative tree projects is that by the very act of becoming a community member to participate, you have to adhere to certain standards, not least the ceding of some 'sovereignty' over the 'territory' that was previously your exclusive domain. In other words, it is no longer just your tree.

Many projects will also have rigorous source requirements, something not to be feared, but embraced, because the more solid the evidence base for your research, the firmer your conclusions will be, and the more agreement you will foster from your collaborators.

i) WikiTree
www.wikitree.com
Wikitree is a free-to-access wiki-based platform (p.66) established in 2008, which seeks to create a single, accurate 'collaborative family tree', rather than hosting individual efforts.

When you register with WikiTree, you initially do so as a 'guest member', at which point you will receive an email from a 'WikiTree greeter', a member who can answer questions you may have about participation within the project.

Having signed up as a guest member, you can dip your toe in the water and upload a GEDCOM file to the site in order to create a 'GEDCOMpare report', which may take a few minutes to produce. This tool allows you to consider other profiles which may already exist on the site that connect to your tree, although many will simply be profiles for people with the same names as ancestors, but unconnected. At this stage, however, you cannot fully import your tree file to the site, or create a tree without adding a GEDCOM file, you can only create a profile page for yourself.

To become more active, you can upgrade your membership to be a 'Family Member' or take things even further to become a 'Wiki Genealogist', with both tiers again free-to-access. To become a Family

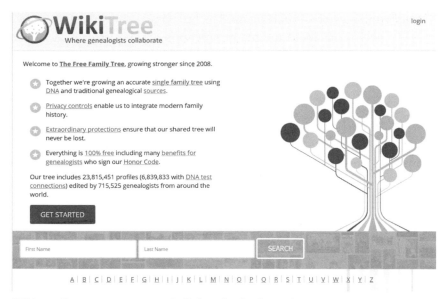

Wikitree allows users to create a 'collaborative family tree'.

Member you must volunteer to collaborate with others on the platform, by providing some basic information about your interest, and a 'Greeter' will soon after confirm your membership. You can request access to work on a particular profile by contacting a Family Member who is a profile page manager for that particular relative, and help to fill in some of the blanks, or alternatively, become a Family Member by being invited by somebody who is already a Wiki Genealogist.

To become a Wiki Genealogist, which will allow you to upload your own GEDCOMs and to be able to gain unlimited rights to create and edit profiles, you must sign up to WikiTree's 'Honor Code', essentially a nine-point series of rules which you agree to abide by throughout your participation.

On WikiTree there is a profile page for each person within a tree, each with its own dedicated URL (p.116) and profile number. The profile page provides an overview of that individual's birth, marriage and death information, as well as noting their immediate family connections, such as their parents, siblings, spouses and descendants. The names for all of these will be presented as hyperlinks, each of which connects to their own dedicated profile page.

Participants collaborating on a profile page can make edits, contact each other through the site's internal messaging system, make public comments, and also interact through the site's Genealogist-to-Genealogist Forum (G2G).

WikiTree takes a bit of getting used to, but it is a powerful collaborative tool. To help learn about the many functions of the platform there is a dedicated WikiTree YouTube channel available, with many detailed guides to help you to learn the ropes.

ii) Geni
www.geni.com
Geni is another platform seeking to create a 'single world family tree'. Created in 2008 and acquired by MyHeritage in 2012, today it offers two tiers of membership: a basic free access subscription or a Pro subscription service, which offers an option to locate matching profiles and to merge them into one single tree.

As with WikiTree and other platforms you can import a GEDCOM file, or build a tree from scratch. The Geni Family Tree can also be used to host projects centred on a particular theme, which can link to profiles of people – for example, there is a project on the RMS Titanic, with background information on its construction and ownership, the passengers who sailed on board, and the crew. The page includes several lists of people as created within the Geni database.

Other features on the platform include a discussion board, and a dedicated blog at **www.geni.com/blog**.

As with WikiTree, there is also a YouTube channel for Geni.com with a small number of tutorial videos which may help.

iii) FamilySearch Family Tree
www.familysearch.org
The FamilySearch website has a free-to-access tree-building platform, with the main tools needed for construction found under the first menu option on the home page, marked 'Family Tree'. A basic introduction is outlined at **www.familysearch.org/home/etb_gettingstarted**, with additional help resources at **www.familysearch.org/help/helpcenter/family-tree**.

Through the 'Tree' and 'Person' menu items you can construct a family tree on the site, and add individual details about a person. Each individual is assigned an ID number upon creation. On the Person tab, any information added is available for all to search and see, although the site notes that if you add details about a living person, that information will be held in a private space – although 'anyone could potentially see the photos, documents, and stories that are attached to this person'.

The Person page has various sub-menu headings. On the main 'Details' page you can add a 'Life Sketch' for each individual, essentially a note-based summary tool to provide a short account of who the person is or was. The 'Vitals' section invites you to add the basic vital details on births, marriages, deaths etc.), whilst 'Other information' allows users to input details for a further range of customisable criteria, including military service, immigration, religious affiliation, and even a 'title of nobility' if so burdened. The 'Family Members' section at the bottom of a page is a smaller version of the family tree for that person, noting spouses, parents and children.

Each box that invites you to input a factual detail also allows you to note the 'Reason This Information Is Correct'. If somebody wishes to challenge your assertion over a particular detail, they will at least see on what basis you have made such a conclusion, but it also permits users an opportunity to think about what is being added: is it right?

Further headings under the Person page menu include a handy 'Time Line' function to view events in a chronological order, a 'Sources' page, a 'Collaborate' page into which you can post questions for future visitors to perhaps answer, and a 'Memories' page on to which you can store photos, documents, stories and even audio recordings.

The right-hand side of the Person page lists various functions that can help. The 'Search Records' area allows you to search the holdings of partner sites for potential records of interest, as well as through FamilySearch itself. The 'Tools' section allows you to further search for individuals in other family trees on the platform, whilst the 'Print' section provides a range of family tree charts and reports for printing.

One key thing to note on the Person page is that a list of 'Latest Changes' that you have made to your tree will be noted on the right-hand side of the page also (a list of recent changes is also viewable from the 'Recent' tab on the Family Tree main menu), which can be viewed by anyone reaching your page. User-submitted family trees are also searchable through the 'Find' menu option. If you find a person that you believe to be a family member, you can integrate them to your tree by using the 'Merge by ID' function in the Tools menu to the right-hand side of the page.

It is equally possible for other people to interact and make changes to your page; if this happens, their name will be noted as the person who made the change, and you can then contact them to discuss further. FamilySearch has a blog page entitled 'How to Contact Other Users – Working Together on the Family Tree' at **www.familysearch.org/blog/ en/contacting-other-users/** which explains the main ways to collaborate on a tree, but it does also note the following potential risks in so doing:

Occasionally, you may notice that a user has submitted multiple errors. Some users aren't as experienced or knowledgeable as others. Some may not have complete or accurate information. FamilySearch welcomes everyone who wants to help grow the Family Tree and hopes that more experienced researchers can help willing learners improve their contributions.

The site's Help section for the Family Tree feature at **www.familysearch.org/help/helpcenter/family-tree** also has an article entitled 'How can I prevent other people from making inaccurate changes to Family Tree?'

Note also that there is a FamilySearch Family Tree app available for phones and other portable devices. Amongst the additional features facilitated on this is a tool to capture audio recordings, which can be stored in your FamilySearch Memories folders (see p.123).

Chapter 5

DNA: IT'S IN THE BLOOD

One of the most exciting developments over the last few years has been the rapid evolution in the use of our own DNA as a tool for family history research – we are the most primary documents that we will ever encounter, if we are willing to exploit our very selves for our ancestral pursuits. Using DNA testing for genealogical research is the ultimate in crowdsourcing projects, because it specifically relies on our own, truly unique contribution to work, and that of others equally willing to share a little of themselves, towards achieving a singular common family history goal.

DNA stands for deoxyribonucleic acid, and in simple terms, it carries the programming for our cells and bodily functions which shape who we are, and is something we inherit from our parents. We all have many cousins who descend from our direct ancestors, and who carry some of the same DNA as we do, but in most cases we often only know about the cousins who may be closest to us, if even those. By identifying relatives who share bits of the same inherited DNA, and in using our family trees to confirm those relationships, we can sometimes create entirely new sources for our research.

For example, if we have a two times great-grandmother for whom we cannot find a baptismal record or place of birth, and through the use of a DNA test then discover a second cousin who just happens to have inherited the family bible and all the diaries your shared ancestor left behind, that will probably in itself be reward enough for the initial outlay.

In order to fully utilise a DNA test for genealogy purposes, it is not enough to simply take the test, you will also have to upload a family tree file alongside the results, for without the ability to look for cousins in another tester's family tree, your DNA results will simply just reveal a possible breakdown of your ethnicity (p.97). Whilst this may be handy in some circumstances, and whilst it is certainly an angle that the vendors push heavily when marketing their products, from the family historian's point of view it can often be the least interesting aspect of the whole process, not least because of the regular changes made to ethnicity results on each particular platform.

There are, of course, many caveats and considerations to take into account if wishing to pursue a family history DNA test. The following are just a few:

- A DNA test may connect you to a wondrous revelation, but it may equally lead to a shock discovery, such as the fact that you may have been adopted, or that a much loved parent, grandparent, sibling or other relation may not be your biological relative at all.
- The commercial DNA testing companies for family history research are not charities, and it may not necessarily be your best interests that they have at heart, but those of their shareholders or other interested parties. In thinking about taking a test, it is worth considering who actually holds your data, how secure that data might be, and what rights you have to remove yourself from their databases should you later choose to do so.
- Privacy is an issue that connects to the former point, as is the law of unintended consequences. In recent years, for example, some controversy has arisen from the use of DNA genealogy databases by law enforcement firms in the United States to pursue certain cold cases, which have resulted in prosecutions. For some users, that was never the basis on which they agreed to submit their test results to the DNA databases in question, whilst others are fine with this as a development. Various databases have changed their terms and conditions as a consequence, but it is worth making sure that you are aware of the possibility, or not, of such potential developments occurring.
- Some tests may not be suitable for everyone, For example, Ancestry advises that if you have had a bone marrow transplant, you should not take its autosomal DNA test (p.92), because the saliva sample you provide may actually include a mixture of your DNA and that of your donor.

For the more detailed aspects of the science involved in DNA testing, there are far wiser individuals in the world than I who can explain the many different aspects of the world of 'genetic genealogy', as it is labelled.

Useful books on the topic include *The Family Tree Guide to DNA Testing and Genetic Genealogy* by Blaine Bettinger, and *Tracing Your Ancestors Using DNA: A Guide for Family Historians*, by Graham S. Holton, John Cleary, Michelle Leonard, Iain MacDonald and Alisdair F. MacDonald. For the complete beginner, however, this chapter will provide an introduction to the usefulness of DNA testing, and how to pursue it online to locate genetic cousins through some of the resources available.

NB: It should be noted that some DNA testing companies also now offer 'health report' capabilities, suggesting possible illnesses and conditions you may be susceptible to. Life is short enough as it is, and I have never personally had any interest in pursuing these myself ('dammit Jim, I'm a genealogist, not a doctor!'). Such services can also be further explored if of interest but will not be considered here.

DNA tests

Several commercial companies offer DNA tests for genealogical purposes, including FamilyTreeDNA (**www.familytreedna.com**), Ancestry (**www. ancestry.co.uk/dna**), MyHeritage (**www.myheritage.com**), 23andMe (**www.23andme.com**), and LivingDNA (**www.livingdna.com**). Not every company will offer tests for all types of DNA though, with both MyHeritage and Ancestry, for example, only testing for autosomal DNA. The various options available will be discussed from p.96.

After you have taken a test with a provider, you can download the raw data from your result and upload it to other platforms, with some permitting this for free, whilst others charge a small fee. It is usually a good idea to do this, as each platform has a different subscriber base, meaning that you can make further matches with additional cousins who may not have tested with the same company you did. However, before doing so, make sure that you are happy with the terms and conditions (p.17) of the additional platforms that you might wish to add your results to.

There are several different types of DNA that we inherit, each with their own uses for family historians. The following is a brief overview of each in turn.

i) Y-chromosome DNA (Y-DNA)

When a child is born, its sex is determined by the sex chromosomes. A male child inherits an X-chromosome from his mother and a Y-chromosome from his father, whilst a female child inherits an X-chromosome from each, and therefore does not carry a Y-chromosome.

As well as inheriting a Y-chromosome from his father, a son also traditionally inherits his surname, which theoretically means that both the surname and the Y-DNA chromosome should be passed down the centuries together on the male line. As many distant male cousins will be descended from a common ancestor, the Y-DNA test is therefore a perfect test to locate these cousins, so long as results are added into a database with a corresponding family tree showing the male lines of each tester going back. It is for this reason that Y-DNA tests are especially popular with researchers carrying out surname studies (see p.10). It is sometimes the case, however, that this passing down the generations together of a surname and Y-DNA does

The author's father, Colin Paton, carries the same Y-DNA chromosome as the author – as inherited from his father, and his father before that.

not happen in this predicted manner, for example, when a child born from an unmarried mother adopts her surname instead of its father's, or if an adopted child takes on the surname of an adoptive parent.

A positive property of Y-DNA for genealogists is that it slightly mutates down the generations, but at a rate which can be measured. This means that even if no tree has been uploaded by a match, you can still try to predict how closely a prospective cousin may relate to you, albeit not exactly, through a measure termed 'genetic distance'. If such a cousin seems a particularly close match, you can then contact them for further information.

When taking a Y-DNA test, you will be asked to provide a saliva sample, which you then return by post to the testing company. Various marker points (known as alleles) within the DNA of your Y-chromosome are then examined, and at each point a numerical value is noted, which note the number of times a repeated piece of DNA code has been found at that particular location (known as STRs, or short tandem repeats). The testers will also determine which branch of the population your Y-DNA belongs to, known as a 'haplogroup'.

For everyday use, all you need to know is that your Y-DNA basically consists of a list of these marker points that have been examined (the value then recorded beside each of them), and the haplogroup, which you then compare with the results of another tester, to try to find as many matches as possible. The following is an example of three of the thirty-seven markers examined on my own Y-DNA chain, when I tested many years ago with FamilyTreeDNA (see p.105):

Marker	Value
DYS393	13
DYS390	23
DYS19 (DYS394)	11

Etc...

Just think of each as 'point 1' on your DNA chain, 'point 2' on the chain, etc. The more of the marker points that can be examined in a test, the more accurate a match can be made with your genetic cousins, but also the more expensive will be the test. My Y-DNA haplogroup is further noted by the company as being R-M269.

Whilst only men can take a Y-DNA test, women can still ask their fathers, brothers, uncles or some other male relative to take one on their behalf in order to follow their paternal ancestry.

ii) **Mitochondrial DNA (mtDNA),**

Mitochondrial DNA or mtDNA is a type of DNA found within our cells which can only pass from a mother to a child. So whilst I have some mtDNA as inherited from my mother, I have not passed this on to my two sons, whose mtDNA is instead inherited from their mother. As a mother inherits mtDNA from her mother, and she in turn from her mother, etc., its main genealogical property is that it follows the maternal line going back through time.

One problem for researchers, however, is that the names of women on a maternal line going back usually change from generation to generation, so you cannot easily compare your results with other

Although the author has the same mtDNA as his mother (as she in turn inherited from her mother), he has not passed this on to his two sons.

people in a surname project in the same way that you could with a Y-DNA database. Another problem is that mtDNA mutates at a much slower rate between generations than Y-DNA, meaning that many people will seemingly have the same profile for several centuries, making it difficult to identify where an ancestral connection may have taken place.

Whilst mtDNA can be tested for, and occasionally does have some use for ancestral research – most famously as a tool that was used to confirm the discovered remains of Richard III in a Leicester-based car park on 25 August 2012 (see **www.richardiii.net/7.1_LFR_faqs.php**) – it is not a test that most of us can really do a great deal with, at least for the time being.

iii) Autosomal DNA

In recent years, autosomal DNA testing has become a truly massive industry, with the biggest selling point being that everyone can be tested, men and women, and with most people able to make cousin connections fairly quickly. This type of DNA comes from our autosomes, i.e. the other twenty-two chromosomes that each parent has which do not determine our sex (i.e. the X and Y chromosomes). Your autosomal DNA comprises twenty-two autosomal pairs, with one autosome from each parent in each pair.

Autosomal DNA is passed down from both parents to their children, with roughly 50 per cent obtained from each. This means that you have about half of the DNA that was inherited by your father from his parents, and half of the DNA inherited by your mother from hers. Your brothers and sisters will carry a similar mix, although the actual bits that you have inherited from your parents will differ to those inherited by your siblings – if this was not the case, you and your siblings would all be clones (as, is essentially the case with identical twins, triplets, etc.).

Each parent in turn has inherited their autosomal DNA from each of their respective parents, which in simplistic terms means that your DNA profile consists of about a quarter from each grandparent. The further back in your tree you go, the smaller the amount of the DNA that you inherit from earlier ancestors. In theory this means that you should have about an eighth of your DNA from each great-grandparent, and a sixteenth of the DNA from each great-great-grandparent, and so on.

Now imagine that a small amount of the bit of DNA that you have inherited from an ancestor has also been inherited by a distant cousin – perhaps a second, third, or fourth cousin. If you have placed your results into a database and your distant cousin has done the same thing, the database should be able to flag up which tiny part of your whole DNA profile matches with that of your cousin. If you have hosted your family tree online going back several generations and your distant cousin has done the same thing, at some point you are both going to have the same common ancestor. So long as both of your family trees are accurate, then it will be easy to identify exactly who this is. You can then communicate with each other and collaborate, to discuss what you each know about each of your lines that descended from your shared progenitor.

So that is the basic theory – but it was never going to be quite as easy as that! In truth, we do not actually inherit such equal proportions of our ancestors' autosomal DNA. You inherit about 50 per cent of your DNA from your mum, and 50 per cent from your dad. It may then be, however, that you actually have about 29 per cent DNA from one grandfather, 24 per cent from the other, perhaps 26 per cent from one granny and just 21 per cent from your other granny. This is because of the way that the DNA recombines when it is passed down to a child. As you go further back, it is actually possible within a few generations to have inherited absolutely no DNA whatsoever from certain ancestral lines, and yet find that one of your siblings has. Biologically, we are quite literally *not* the sum of all our parts – the DNA of many ancestors has bid us farewell long before we were even born. In other words, there is a difference between your genealogical ancestry, and your genetic ancestry.

It is for this reason that people often test not only themselves, but as many siblings, aunts and uncles, and even grandparents, as possible, in order to try to maximise the amount of ancestral DNA that they can identify which has been passed on from earlier generations.

Within a family, the children of a couple will each have inherited different mixes of autosomal DNA from their parents.

The following is a basic example of why testing just beyond yourself in your family is a good idea. I took an autosomal DNA test with AncestryDNA (p.97) in 2017. Once I had tested, I soon discovered hundreds of cousin matches to me, all with small parts of DNA that we had inherited from common ancestors, but with only some having accompanying family trees online. This meant that for many matches I was not sure if they connected to me through a common ancestor within my maternal ancestry or my paternal ancestry. How was I to narrow it down?

My mother unfortunately passed away in 2013, and was thus unable to be tested, but a few years later her Australian-based brother did kindly agree to take a test. When his results came through, I was then able to identify some of those matches as being on my mum's side of the family, as the DNA of my uncle had come from my mother's parents. However, because my uncle and my mum did not share exactly the same bits of DNA that they had inherited from their parents, this still left me with a problem. Despite a large number of the matches I had in my tree now being identified as connected to cousins on my maternal line, the remaining matches that were not shared by both my uncle and myself were not necessarily just on my father's side. The problem was that some of those unidentified matches may still have been with distant cousins who connected to bits of DNA that my mother had inherited from her parents, which her brother, my uncle, had not.

There was only way to conclusively identify which half of my DNA matches were on my father's side, and which were on my mother's, and that was to ask my father to do a test. When he agreed in 2019, his results conclusively showed which half of my matches were from his side of the family, for any who matched both my father and me were clearly cousins who connected to us on the paternal side of my family. By default, this in turn meant that most of the remaining unidentified matches had to be on my mother's side – even those for which there was no match with my uncle. (The small caveat here is that some very distant matches may be false positives – but again, let's stick with the big picture!)

So is it worth the effort? For this genealogist, absolutely. I have made many connections with researchers around the world, and in some cases, have confirmed certain hypotheses about from whom I have descended, and from where, and in others I have discovered entire family branches that emigrated from Scotland and Ireland, which have since added considerably to my understanding of my past families.

In one example, I met a person many years ago at a conference in Brisbane, Australia, who audibly gasped when I mentioned the name of an ancestor, Jackson Currie, during a talk I was giving. She had an ancestor of the same name, who although not the same person, was from the same part of Northern Ireland as my person. Following my DNA test, I discovered that she too had taken a test, and that we were in fact connected, and with other members of the family also showing up as matches, we were able to work out how. Just for good measure, I have also established recently that I have a shared DNA connection with another speaker from that very same conference, with a common ancestor from a County Antrim parish in Northern Ireland, who we are now trying to identify together.

In another example, I had long suspected that there was something not quite right about a relative noted in the Scottish censuses, who was stated to be a daughter of my Irish great-great-grandparents George and Jane. The daughter, called Ellen, was noted in censuses to have been born in about 1875 in Ireland. My problem was not only that no birth record could be found for her, I was also suspicious that her parents would have been almost 50 when she was born – not quite impossible, but certainly enough to set off my genealogical 'spidey sense'! I did locate a potential birth record for an Ellen in 1875, but to a mother called Frances, and in the area of County Fermanagh where George and Jane had originated. Through my DNA connections I later established that this was in fact the correct Ellen, and that following her birth, her mother Frances had emigrated to the United States, and left her daughter to be raised by her grandparents George and Jane, who were Frances' parents, and who shortly after moved to Scotland.

The measurement of how closely related you might be to a distant cousin is reckoned in what are known as 'centimorgans', or 'cM' for short. With my father, we share 3450 cM of autosomal DNA, whereas my uncle and I share a smaller amount, at 1541 cM. The smaller the number, the more distant the relationship is likely to be, although there can be complications in this also, for example, through 'endogamy', which is where intermarriage in earlier generations (when cousins marry) leads to you having the same pair of ancestors on more than one line, thus affecting the amount of DNA passed down. When an unknown match appears on your list with a very high match rate in centimorgans, this can produce some particularly extraordinary revelations in your tree.

Probably the most sensational find I have made in recent years has been the discovery of a second cousin, who contacted me after we showed as a potential match, and who shared a very high amount of autosomal DNA at 314 cM. His mother had been born illegitimately over a century ago, and he had never known who his grandfather was. When he initially contacted me I was unable to immediately identify where he fitted in, but testing my father opened other doors to our research, and through the analysis of his shared matches, and other resources, we eventually narrowed it down to the correct candidate and confirmed that we are indeed second cousins.

But once again, a word of caution. Whilst the tests have been personally very useful for my research, I know many people who have had some exceptional shocks to the system after testing, revealing parents, grandparents, and other relationships, to not be what had been long believed and researched. Autosomal testing can be a popular genealogical lottery, but not everyone may necessarily emerge as a winner.

iv) X-chromosome DNA (X-DNA)
The X-chromosome is a sex chromosome, along with the Y-chromosome, which can determine our biological sex, with a woman having two X-chromosomes to determine her sex, whereas a man has an X-chromosome and a Y-chromosome.

For a man, the X-chromosome can only be an inherited from his mother, whereas a woman will inherit an X-chromosome from each of her two parents. This leads to a unique inheritance pattern of X-DNA for both men and women. A man's X-chromosome can only come from his mother, which in turn may come from either of his two maternal grandparents. By contrast, a woman inherits a particular X-chromosome from either of her two parents, which in turn may have come from either of her maternal grandparents, or her paternal grandmother, but not from her paternal grandfather!

Because of these unique ways in which the X-chromosome can be inherited, testing of X-chromosome DNA can be useful to an extent to help narrow down the field if an autosomal DNA match is made with a distant relative.

The testing of X-DNA is not carried out independently but as part of an autosomal DNA test. It should be noted that although most testing platforms will illustrate which ancestral matches share X-DNA, at the time of writing, Ancestry does not.

Testing platforms
Many companies provide DNA testing for genealogical purposes, with several unique features. The following are the most widely used at present within the UK and Ireland:

i) AncestryDNA
www.ancestry.co.uk/dna

Ancestry's DNA platform exclusively tests for autosomal DNA. Whilst some people will only test with Ancestry to work out what they believe their ethnicity is, the site becomes a considerably more powerful tool for cousin hunting when a tester's family tree is uploaded (see p.72) and then linked to his or her DNA results. Users can do a test with Ancestry if they have a basic free account, but in order to make contact with matches, you will need a paid subscription. At the time of writing the platform offers three main features to those who have tested.

An 'Ethnicity Estimate' allows you to 'discover your DNA Story' by trying to identify your ethnic origin after matching your DNA result to tens of thousands of samples from over a thousand regions (called a 'reference panel'). The ethnicity measure (technically the 'admixture' estimate) is of course only based on your genetic ancestry, and as noted earlier, your genetic tree only tells part of the story when compared to your genealogical tree. In an early advert run by Ancestry in 2015, a tester was depicted saying how his results showed his ethnic origin to be 52 per cent from Scotland and Ireland, instead of his expected German ancestry, with the tester gleefully reporting 'I traded in my lederhosen for a kilt!'

As Ancestry takes on more and more DNA subscribers, however, the quality and accuracy of these reference panels increases across time, and so you will find that your stated ethnicity will be revised from time to

As with other DNA platforms, Ancestry will provide an estimate of ethnicity. Reassuringly for the author, his results agree with his Scottish and Irish credentials! As more people are tested, the estimates will evolve over time.

time as a consequence, not just with the percentages but with the possible introduction of new or revised 'Community' groups – abrupt fashion changes based on DNA results alone might therefore be ill-advised. Where this ethnicity feature can be useful, however, is for those who may have been adopted, and who may have no idea where in the world their parents came from, as it might help to narrow down to a particular region or community.

The real business end of the platform for most family historians is the 'DNA Matches' section, where Ancestry flags up people with whom you share DNA, so long as the match is 8cM or higher, and how many segments of DNA you share. If your relative has a family tree hosted on its site, Ancestry will identify a common ancestor and allow you to see exactly how you are related.

If you do flag up as a match, you can view your connection's tree, and contact them through Ancestry's internal messaging system. Once you know on which line your ancestor connects, you can also add them to a group that you have created for that line to help you retrieve the match more easily in the future. If your cousin has uploaded a family tree but has not linked it to his or her DNA results, you can still visit their tree, but any obvious connections will not be instantly flagged up. Some users do also have a tree uploaded which is in fact connected to the DNA result, but which has been set to private. In such cases the number of people within that tree is noted, but you will need to contact the owner if you wish to find out more.

The one big caveat here is that for this to work, your tree has to be accurate, as does that of your cousin. No ifs, no buts – it has to be 100 per cent accurate. Sadly, not everyone has an accurate tree online. You will therefore almost certainly at some point find a match with someone with a suggested common ancestor that is in fact just wrong – but this will not be Ancestry's fault, it is simply trying to help with the best information available to it. In such a case, whilst the suggested connection may be wrong, you are still connected, and you can still look at other lines to try to determine how.

If no tree has been uploaded it may be difficult to establish how you are related. One very useful feature that Ancestry does offer, however, is the ability to view 'Shared Matches', namely people with whom you both connect. The family trees of these shared connections may yield clues as to how you relate – for example, if a user with no tree matches to five distant cousins, all of whom have the same three times great-grandparents, that would be a fair starting point as to where your cousin's anonymous connection lies.

The third main feature on Ancestry is a facility it calls 'ThruLines'. The stated aim of this tool is to suggest how you might be related to others through common ancestors, using the fact that you share DNA connections with distant cousins and that they have uploaded family trees to their accounts that they have linked to their DNA results. In essence, it shows a list of ancestors that you have identified in your tree, and states the number of possible connections that it suggests you could have to each, which it graphically illustrates when clicking on a particular ancestor's name by tracing the lines of suggested descendants from that common ancestor, including one to yourself.

Note that ThruLines can also be accessed by two other methods. From the 'DNA Matches' page, if an ancestor is shown as having a 'Common Ancestor', then you can click on this link; on the next page, click on the 'View Relationship' link for the suggested common ancestor in the left-hand column, which will take you through to the proposed ThruLines match. Alternatively, if you access your main family tree diagram on Ancestry (via the 'Trees' link on the home page), any match that has a suggested ThruLines link will have a small blue circle at the top left of that individual's box on the tree. Click on the individual's box, and at the bottom you will then be invited to directly view the suggested ThruLines connections.

It is important to note that if ThruLines suggests that you are connected to somebody, then that is what it is giving you – a suggestion, nothing more, and nothing less – and you may really need to take some

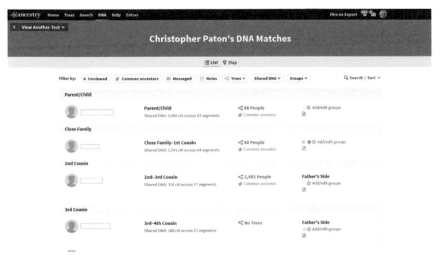

Ancestry lists matches in order of the closest relationship, and can identify possible common ancestors for two matching cousins, if they each have trees uploaded. (Names of relatives protected for privacy.)

of these offerings with a pinch of salt. Again, the key issue here is the accuracy of the trees that have been uploaded. Nevertheless, for more recent connections, which are much easier to verify from documentary resources, it can be a very useful tool indeed. Note that for ThruLines to work, hosted trees must contain at least 3-4 generations back from the tester, and that it will only work with a maximum of seven generations.

Where Ancestry does fall short is that it does not offer a facility called a chromosome browser (p.103), which can be useful in determining exactly which bits of a person's DNA are shared by a tester and his or her cousins. Ancestry cites privacy concerns for not implementing this as a tool, but it is possible to download the raw data from your AncestryDNA test and to add it to another platform which does offer this. However, the sheer user friendliness of Ancestry's platform design on all other fronts has made it one of the most popular DNA platforms around.

ii) MyHeritage DNA
www.myheritage.com/dna
The DNA testing platform at MyHeritage is one of the company's stronger offerings from a UK perspective. Like Ancestry, MyHeritage tests for autosomal DNA only (although it unfortunately does not flag up any accompanying X-DNA results), and has an equally substantial database of matches from around the world. Whilst offering much in terms of the ability to link you to genetic cousins, it also has a few other tools and capabilities that differ markedly to those of Ancestry.

The 'DNA' tab is found on the main menu at the top of the home page, and from within this are options in the sub-menu to either take a test through the company itself or to upload your raw data results from another tester. The 'How it Works' menu option provides some background information from a technical viewpoint should you wish to learn more before ordering a kit.

Once you have your test results on the system, the first four options on the DNA menu offer capabilities in four main areas, through which you can move on the DNA results page via a series of tabs a little further down the page.

The 'Overview' screen will provide a brief summary of what it surmises your ethnicity to be, which is then followed by a 'DNA Matches' section summarising how many matches you have; this is broken down to 'Close family' members, 'Extended family' members, and 'Distant relatives'. A 'Locations' map also shows where in the world your genetic cousins are based, which is then followed by an 'Ethnicities' table, providing an 'ethnicity distribution of your DNA Matches'. Whilst this can be interesting, you will move on from it fairly quickly to the next tabs, which begin to address your results in more detail.

The 'Ethnicity Estimate' screen allows you to see how MyHeritage has judged your ethnicity to be defined. If you have tested on another platform, you will immediately notice that the various individual ethnic groups that your DNA is stated to reveal may differ somewhat substantially from those on the other site on which you have your results hosted. It is not that MyHeritage is any more right or any more wrong on this, it is simply a matter of how it is has created its reference populations from the numbers of people testing with its site. So as with any other DNA platform, for the most part take the conclusions with a pinch of salt, and be prepared for potential revisions down the line. The page offers an introductory video to explain what it is trying to depict for you, and a map depicting the areas from which your ancestry is stated to have originated.

By far the real work area is the 'DNA Matches' section. On here you will be presented with details of potential matches, which can be arranged in a variety of orders using the 'Filters' menu option and the 'Sort by' menu. Filters allows you to arrange results by those with online family trees, with a shared surname and with a shared place of origin, and also with connections for who results have been enhanced by MyHeritage's own matching tools, known as 'Theory of Family Relativity' and 'Smart Matches'. You can also narrow down by the locations of where your matches are based, the relationship category that they might fall into (i.e. 'Extended Family' and 'Distant Relatives'), and by 'Ethnicities'. The Sort by menu allows you to rearrange the results based on the amount of 'Shared segments' of DNA, the 'Largest segment', by the 'Full name' of a cousin or by the 'Most recent' results. There is also a magnifying glass symbol which, when clicked on, allows you to search for a name or ancestral surname within a match's family tree, and additional tools for exporting results are found with a menu option behind three vertical dots at the end of the menu bar.

On the main list of results, for any potential cousin match result listed, you will find the name given, an age and location, an estimated relationship and information about the 'DNA Match quality' broken down as the amount of shared DNA in a percentage, the number of shared DNA segments with you, and the size in centimorgans of the largest of these. At the bottom of each summary profile you will also be informed if they have a family tree online, and if so how many people appear within it, and whether each person has any Smart Matches or Theory of Family Relativity connections. To the right of each entry you will find a purple button inviting you to 'Review DNA Match' and if there is a family tree available, a white button providing access to this.

Clicking a particular match takes you to a new page with considerably more detail. You will have an option to contact your new-found cousin, with information on your estimated relationship and DNA Match quality. If MyHeritage believes that it has evidence from your cousin's family tree that are also presented in your tree, these will be highlighted next in a series of 'Shared Matches', which may further help to suggest exactly how you connect. In addition to this, MyHeritage can also present ideas of how it *thinks* you may be connected, via its Theory of Family Relativity projections. This works in a similar way to Ancestry's Thrulines (p.99), suggesting theoretical connections from known information on the site, including online-hosted trees, and other documentary resources (e.g. censuses), on what it thinks your common ancestor might be. Note that if you have imported your tree results from another platform, you will need to pay a small fee to unlock this feature (US$29 at the time of writing).

A list of 'Ancestral Surnames' in your cousin's tree is then presented, alongside a map of 'Ancestral Places'. This is then followed by a list of 'Shared DNA Matches', which will note others to whom you both connect,

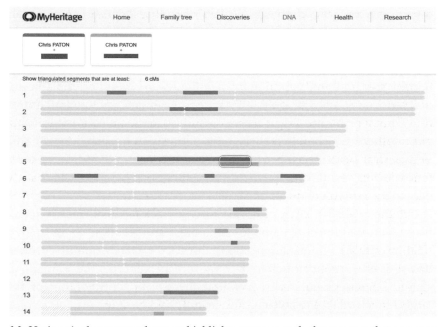

MyHeritage's chromosome browser highlights areas on each chromosome that you may share with other testers. The circled area is the triangulated segment shared by the author and two distant cousins.

and the amounts of DNA that you individually share with that person, both as a percentage and in centimorgans. Some of these matches may have a symbol at the far right of their entry, indicating that MyHeritage has identified a 'triangulated segment' of DNA, in other words a section of DNA that all three of you share. By clicking on this symbol, you will be taken to another page, offering a tool called a 'Chromosome Browser'.

A chromosome browser will graphically show on which of your twenty-two autosomal pairs (p.92) the shared DNA of your matches is located. The areas that all three of you share – the triangulated segment – is ringed off on this image, so for example, you may discover that each of you has a small shared segment on the eighth autosomal pair line. If you are already aware of the ancestry of one of the matches, and know how you connect, but have never heard of the other person, and there is no tree available, the fact that you share such an area of DNA may indicate that this is another distant cousin on the same line – all three of you may have inherited that same bit of DNA from a common ancestor. On the list of Shared DNA Matches it may indicate more than one person who has a triangulated segment, and on the chromosome browser you can examine up to seven cousins at a time to see where your shared DNA overlaps with each other.

Following the Shared DNA Matches box, if your cousin has uploaded a tree, you may also encounter a 'Pedigree Chart' which can helpfully show your match's direct ancestry. Beneath this is another area to explore 'Shared ethnicities', and then another graphic of a chromosome browser just showing the areas of DNA with which you and your cousin overlap.

The final option from the main DNA Results menu page is one marked 'Tools'. In here you will find another link allowing you to access the Chromosome Browser, and an option to access an Ethnicities Map, but another very useful resource within here is the 'AutoClusters' tool, which arranges the results of who you match into a series of 'clusters' who are likely to descend from common ancestors – another very handy way to try to predict how you may be connected to individuals for whom less ancestral documentary information is available.

iii) Living DNA
https://livingdna.com/uk

The UK-based LivingDNA service provides deep ancestry testing for Y-DNA and mtDNA, as well as autosomal DNA testing.

Through its 'Ancestry' page, the Y-DNA and mtDNA results are presented in two sections, Maternal Ancestry and Paternal Ancestry, which will inform users of their particular haplogroups (specific branches of the human population) and display the migration maps of their ancestors back towards the common origin of all human groups in Africa. In my case, for example, my maternal haplogroup is defined at the time of writing as H56a1, thought to have originated some 25,000–30,000 years ago, whilst my paternal haplogroup is noted as R-U106, the 'Germanic branch of the R1b fatherline'! Although mildly interesting, the information as displayed for my Y-DNA and mtDNA results does not actually allow me to make connections with any genetic cousins.

By contrast, the autosomal DNA results do permit a limited means to establish connections with distant cousins, but at the time of writing this is not yet presented in as convenient a manner as found on other autosomal DNA testing platforms. LivingDNA will find matches from other users, and provide them in a list on its 'Family Networks' page (noted as the 'Relatives' menu link), detailing their predicted relationship, the amount of DNA shared in both centimorgans and by percentage, and a means by which to message your potential cousins. At the time of writing, there is as yet no means by which to visually identify a cousin's family tree to try to find out where a connection lies. The site is developing its service, however, and will in time offer improved facilities, including a chromosome browser and other features to help determine such relationship connections.

Where LivingDNA massively trumps its rivals on the autosomal DNA front is in the visual mapping of a user's ethnicity (admixture), with the results broken down in considerably more detail for Britain and Ireland across twenty-one regions. It is able to do so because it uses the results of a long term research initiative started in 2004 called the *People of the British Isles Project* (**www.peopleofthebritishisles.org**), in which volunteers were invited to take a DNA test if they had four grandparents all born within a 50-mile radius. The results created a useful reference panel when published in 2015, to which LivingDNA can now compare any subsequent test results.

So whilst Ancestry tells me through its 'DNA Story' feature (p.97) that I am 65 per cent 'Ireland and Scotland', and 35 per cent 'England, Wales & Northwestern Europe', largely as part of the 'Scottish Lowlands, Northern England & Northern Ireland' community, LivingDNA goes much further in its breakdown. According to LivingDNA, I am 53.1 per cent Northern Ireland and Southwest Scotland, 12.2 per cent Northumbria, 8.7 per cent from the Republic of Ireland, 4.6 per cent Northwest Scotland, 4.5 per cent Aberdeenshire, and even 3 per cent Yorkshire, which ties in with the results found so far from my documentary research. The 8.8 per cent

South Central England, and 3 per cent Welsh are mysteries yet to be resolved, along with the 1.9 per cent Cumbria...!

It should be noted that FindmyPast's DNA offering is in fact a partnership with LivingDNA, and if purchasing a test through FindmyPast you will effectively be redirected to the LivingDNA site to be tested. It is possible to add your results from LivingDNA to a FindmyPast account; in my case, having done so I can see a summary of my ethnicity breakdown on the FindmyPast homepage, but there seems to be little else by way of further benefit – the DNA results do not link to my hosted family tree on the FindmyPast site, negating any possible means to make connections with others who have tested and who have similar accounts, at least at this stage.

iv) FamilyTreeDNA
www.familytreedna.com

Founded in 2000, FamilyTreeDNA is one of the oldest DNA firms testing for genealogical purposes, pioneering the use of Y-DNA testing in particular for surname studies and cousin matching, as well as offering mitochondrial DNA tests.

The company's platform does not just allow you to make connections with individual genetic cousins who match your DNA, it also hosts many unique surname and geographical region-based projects. As someone who tested with them many years ago, for example, I am a subscriber to the North of Ireland DNA Project, the Patton Y-DNA Project, and the Scottish DNA Project, all of which I can access from the home page under the 'myProjects' tab. FamilyTreeDNA now also offers autosomal DNA testing kits, which it calls a 'FamilyFinder' test, with a rapidly growing database of users. I find FamilyTreeDNA to be by far one of the most powerful DNA platforms around, but also one for which there is a massively greater learning curve to really unlock its true potential. Many family history societies run Y-DNA projects using FamilyTreeDNA because of the platform's versatility.

If purchasing a testing kit for the first time, it will have a 'kit number' assigned to it, which will become your username for logging in to the site. In your account settings, you can also name a 'beneficiary' who can take over your account, including your kit and any remaining DNA samples, after you have passed away (see p.19).

The home page is a fairly cluttered affair, but at the top you will see four main essential menu options:

- **Home** – this option does what it says on the tin, and brings you back to the Home page or 'dashboard' when you stray elsewhere on the site. There is a lot on this page, and it can at times feel a bit like information overload, but you can rearrange the layout to prioritise the areas you will more frequently access.
- **MyDNA** – this tab allows you to quickly access menu items for both the FamilyFinder test pages and the Y-DNA pages. Most of these options can also be accessed from panels on the Home page itself.
- **MyTree** – in this section you can upload a family tree GEDCOM file (p.69) or create a new tree from scratch. One useful function here is that you can actually indicate DNA matches with individuals in your tree, and through the 'Tree Management' link at the top right of the page you can keep a list of these matches with their contact details. You can also export the tree using the 'Share Tree' tab at the top right of the page.
- **MyProjects** – from here you can search for, and join, surname and geographic region projects utilising Y-DNA test results.

For all questions concerning the company's practices, there is a Learning Centre accessible in the top right corner of the Home page, by clicking on your kit number and selecting the relevant item from the drop-down menu. This can also be accessed from a link at the very bottom of the page, as can the site's Help section.

Within the 'Autosomal DNA' section on the dashboard, you can access several handy menu items, displaying the names of your genetic cousins with a summary of the amount of DNA you share, the relationship range that this may indicate, the size of the largest block of DNA (in centimorgans), whether you also share a match with your X-DNA, if a link is confirmed on a family tree, the exact relationship you have with that relative and some ancestral names on their tree. By the names of each cousin you may see an image of them (if they have added one to their profile), and there are tools to allow you to email them, to make a note about their results, and to view their tree, if they have one. If you wish to try to find matches for a particular surname, you can type this in also to look for targeted branches of your family.

At the far left of each match's entry you will find a tick box. If you click on those for potential matches of interest (up to a maximum of seven), you can compare their DNA profiles with your own by using the 'Chromosome Browser' function at the top of the page, in order to determine exactly which bits of DNA you might actually share. If you share a segment of DNA on your first chromosome, for example, then

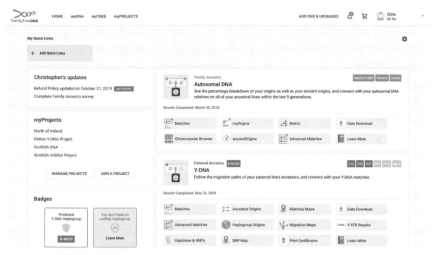

FamilyTreeDNA offers many possibilities, but there is a considerable learning curve involved to fully utilise the tools available.

if others are later found to also have that same piece of DNA in their profile, it is possible that you are related through the same ancestral line. Another tool that can help is the 'In Common With' and 'Not In Common With' options at the top which allow you to find others who may or may not share DNA with yourself and other identified cousins (similar to Ancestry's 'Shared Matches' and MyHeritage's 'Shared DNA Matches' tools). One further tool that allows you to quickly compare if individuals on your match list are related to each other is the 'Matrix' tool, with which you can select up to ten people, and then see in a chart form who relates to whom.

The 'Origins' menu option basically takes you to a map to show you where your ethnicity is deemed to come from, albeit based on twenty-four reference groups from around the world. My results, at the time of writing, show me to be 78 per cent British Isles, 11 per cent West and Central Europe, and 12 per cent Southeast Europe – a far cry from the detail suggested by LivingDNA (p.103).

The Y-DNA results section offers a similar array of tools. You can search for matches within the whole FamilyTree Y-DNA database or within projects that you have joined. You can also select the number of markers you wish to match to (the more markers, the greater the accuracy), and search for matches by surname. Various other tools include a migration map for your surname's haplogroup, and a handy 'Advanced Matches' search tool that permits you to search for potential matches by combining those who share autosomal DNA, Y-DNA and X-DNA.

v) 23andMe

www.23andme.com/en-gb

23andMe offers DNA testing facilities for Y-DNA, mtDNA and autosomal testing. Whilst it does not facilitate the hosting or upload of a user's family tree, autosomal DNA matches can still be made with genetic cousins who share some of your segments, with suggested potential relationships noted.

Additional services, such as DNA testing for health risks, are also provided.

Exporting results to other platforms

In addition to offering tests, some of the DNA platforms will also allow you to import your 'raw data' results from another tester, as a means to lure you towards other services that they might offer. If you are happy with the terms and conditions of such secondary sites, and with their privacy guarantees, it can be immensely useful to do so, for the simple fact that you might make further connections with genetic cousins who have only hosted their results on the single platform through which they tested.

Having tested with Ancestry a few years ago, I subsequently exported my raw data file and uploaded it to FamilyTreeDNA, MyHeritage and LivingDNA. In doing so, I was able to get a much better understanding of my ethnicity/admixture results from LivingDNA, whilst many cousins, who are not hosted on Ancestry, have been found subsequently through both FamilyTreeDNA and MyHeritage. (In fact, through FamilyTreeDNA I have been stunned to learn in the last couple of years that I am a distant cousin to two professional genealogist friends, one based in Australia, the other in Scotland!) In addition, by adding my results to these other sites, I have been able to utilise further tools on them that are not available on Ancestry, most notably their chromosome browsers and matrix tools (p.107), which Ancestry does not offer but which further allow me further options for the analysis of my prospective matches.

By downloading the raw data of your test, you can also add the results to other platforms which do not carry out tests but which can still provide additional means to find cousins. GEDMatch (**www.gedmatch. com**), for example, freely permits users the option to upload raw data and a family tree to its site, where the results can be compared to others within its database to find matches. A subscription tier is also available, with some additional tools to help users analyse results. At the time of writing, GEDMatch accepts uploads of data from AncestryDNA, MyHeritageDNA, FamilyTreeDNA and 23andMe, with a useful video on how to sign up and set up a user profile available at **https://youtu.be/ id7JJ1NoTNk**.

Once in, various other useful videos can be accessed from the main menu to take you through the site's many features, as well as the platform's own 'GEDMatch Wiki'. As with FamilyTreeDNA, it takes a bit of time to learn about the true potential of what it can do for you, but it may well be time well worth investing, depending on your research goals.

Another site that really allows you to get creative, and which injects a bit of fun into DNA research, is Jonny Perl's DNA Painter (**https:// dnapainter.com**). This site allows you to create a map to help visualise the bits of your chromosomes that you share with other genetic cousins, as discovered through the main testing and results-hosting platforms.

If each ancestor in your family tree chart is assigned a colour, the chromosomal map on DNA Painter can basically show you which bits of your twenty-two autosome pairs come from each ancestor – although it takes time to work out which bit goes where, depending on how many genetic cousins you can confirm as being related to you. It may well become a little addictive, but once you have managed to build up your own chromosome map, you can then further use it to predict how other people might be related to you. A useful introduction to the site is explained by Jonny himself in a webinar at **https://familytreewebinars. com/download.php?webinar_id=955**.

The site also provides access to a range of other useful resources. These include the 'What are the Odds?' tool, which 'lets you use the amounts

Jonny Perl's DNA Painter site provides a lot of fun in allowing users to paint their own chromosomal maps, based on matches with genetic cousins.

of DNA you share with multiple matches to help figure out where you might fit into their tree', and the 'Shared cM Tool' created by genetic genealogist Blaine Bettinger (**https://thegeneticgenealogist.com**); this can help you to predict what possible relationships may exist between two genetic cousins based on the amount of centimorgans they share in their DNA, from your immediate parents and siblings to potential relatives as far back as eighth cousins.

Chapter 6

SHARING AND PRESERVING STORIES

Whilst we endeavour to carry out our ancestral research using many online and offline tools, and to manage the vast amounts of data that we might find, the ultimate aim for any ancestral research project is very simple – to tell a story. No matter how great your research is, no matter how many hours you put in, the greatest skill of all in the family history world is to not just be able to make what you find accessible to others, but to make others want to read it, and to perpetuate that story for future generations.

Many years ago, before I became a genealogist for a living, I worked in the television industry as a documentary maker for both the BBC and

TV is not that glamorous – the author earning his stripes as a researcher and 'reflector boy' on the 1996 BBC series War Walks!

Scottish Television Enterprises. With my colleagues, I would toil for many months to gather in all sorts of research, carry out preliminary visits to potential contributors and filming locations, and after various written drafts come up with a script that I hoped would convey the story I wished to tell. I would then carry out the filming and try to paint in that script with contributor interviews and images, and work afterwards with an editor to try to shape the material into something that an audience might wish to watch, imbued with facts, stories and emotion. The end goal was to hope that the viewers would agree that it would most certainly be worth giving up half an hour from their busy lives and schedules to watch what I had produced with my colleagues.

When it comes to my family history research, I try to do exactly the same thing, albeit with a much reduced budget! But ultimately the process is very similar indeed – I carry out family history research, shape the story that emerges, and transmit an end product, by any number of different ways in which I think my relatives or potential clients might engage. The findings follow the considerations required by the Genealogical Proof Standard (p.12), and are always open to challenge.

If there is one difference, it is perhaps that the end product within the genealogical world can be revised repeatedly, rewritten as new facts emerge and new conclusions drawn with each new finding. In family history, the story never ends, but we can certainly share our understanding of it at various points within our lives, and leave our conclusions for others to enjoy and expand upon or challenge long after we have gone.

Conveying the message

As discussed earlier in the book, you can convey genealogical information to a wider audience in a number of ways. The use of family history software (p.69), in particular, can actually help to convey such information in a report-based format at the click of a button. This can be a very effective method to collate everything into a generation-by-generation-themed document, with sources cited and relationships highlighted. However, such reports can be a little dry and formulaic, and if the intent is for this to be the one and only way of passing on the family story, it may be something that is proudly displayed as a trophy, but without actually being read.

Ultimately what you want to do in a family history report is to try to pass on a little bit about the characters of the people that you wish to introduce to your readers. It is certainly possible to amend some automatically generated reports, perhaps by exporting them to a text-based file format and typing in your own added extra comments and context, or perhaps by utilising the notes fields in the software to add in some extra details, fun anecdotes and more.

There are other ways to try to convey such stories, however, involving just a little more creativity.

Creative writing

When wishing to share your ancestral stories, there are several factors to consider, and many ways to shape the content.

i) What stories do you wish to tell?

When you research your family history, you will uncover an incredible amount of information about some ancestors, and not so much for others. For those who are well documented, the story may well write itself, but if your ancestor is not so well recorded, that does not necessarily mean that they were 'boring' or are unworthy of your efforts. Having an 'ag lab' (agricultural labourer) in the tree is in no way the end of the world!

There are many possible ways that you can tell a story. You might wish to write about a specific incident within your ancestry that involved many members. A few years after I started to research my family tree, for example, I made the shocking discovery that an ancestor of mine, Janet Rogers (nee Henderson) had been murdered on a Perthshire farm in 1866. I found so much material relating to the case, from newspaper accounts, trial papers, and more, that I initially tried to transcribe the lot on to my family history website, thinking it to be a great way to share what had happened.

It was not long, however, before I realised that I was essentially creating a data dump of material online, dominating my website with lots of repetition from different sources, which was making it difficult and tedious to reveal the tale of what had actually happened. I therefore wrote an article about it for a family history magazine, and recounted the incident within 1,500 words. I found the process so much fun that I decided that there really was a much bigger story to tell, and in time turned all that I had found into a book, not originally intended for publication, but as a private endeavour for me to pass on to my two boys.

A coincidental investigation by the BBC soon changed that approach, after it sought to track down information about cold cases in the UK, and discovered that my ancestor's murder was in fact Scotland's longest unsolved case by a modern police force, and quite possibly within the whole UK. This created what is known as a 'peg' in the media, something to hang the interest of others on to, beyond the interest of my sons. I therefore contacted a publisher, who happily agreed to produce a print edition of my book, followed by an e-book version. On the back of this, I was subsequently contacted by a few distant cousins, including some still living close by to where the incident occurred.

Of course, not all our stories may be quite big enough to fill a book! You may have some information about certain individuals, which on its own may be an interesting anecdote but which could still contribute to a much bigger picture. You could, perhaps, write a generic article entitled 'My Family in the First World War', and explain how different branches of your family contributed to the war effort, with some perhaps seeing active service overseas, whilst others contributed to the home front, in reserved occupations such as coal mining and shipbuilding, or in specific wartime roles, such as munitions manufacturing.

You may also have a particular individual within your tree, inspiring you from beyond the grave, for whom a biographical account may be an aspiration. On my future 'to do list', for example, is the story of an uncle who worked as a physician for many years in nineteenth-century Perthshire, who has inspired me on many fronts.

ii) Who are your readers?

When writing about your family history, are you writing your account for your immediate loved ones, or are you seeking to engage with a wider readership? The reason why this is important to consider is that the wider you seek to share your account, the more you may have to explain some of the very key basics of what you are talking about.

For example, if you have a story to share with your family from Croydon, which has been based for several generations in Croydon, and which knows every, brick, wall, park and road in Croydon, you may not have to explain a great deal about Croydon to your family in Croydon! For a wider audience around the world, however, you may need to add a little more contextual information about the environment in which your family story is based.

iii) What voice are you using?

This is something I regularly have to deal with as a writer, with the 'voice' written with very much based on whether I am writing for myself or on behalf of someone else. How you choose to write your accounts will very much affect the relationship between you as the writer and those who you hope will read your content.

Whatever way you might choose to tell a story, the very way that you do so will involve subjective choices. As was the case when I worked in television, twenty people could make twenty documentaries about the same event, and every one of those programmes would be completely different, because each would be a contributing factor to how their version of that story would be told.

One of the most obvious ways that this will manifest itself is by the very 'voice' that you use when you write. If I write a story as myself, do I write it as I would speak, with my Ulster accent and local language that would barely make sense to anyone other than those who come from the same area ('hauld yer horses, ye mad buck eejit hallion ye, but that's a fair craic, so it is!'), or do I write in a more neutral, received dialect, understood by many more people, but perhaps taking away a little of the local character? Am I writing in a manner in which the readership will understand that what they are digesting is very much an understanding that I have of a series of events, or am I trying to be more neutral or authoritative in conveying the details of those events? Just what is my relationship to the events in question, and how am I influencing the narrative by what I leave out as much as I leave in? Am I writing as a participant to something that I myself have witnessed or discovered, in a first person style as a participant observer ('I saw the event happen'), or in a more impartial documentary-based manner, as given by a narrator in the third person ('the event happened')?

Am I even writing from my perspective at all? In the past, I have been commissioned to write articles, for example, on behalf of a magazine or online platform where the object is very much not to tell the story from my point of view at all, but to write as if I am the voice of the magazine or the platform in question. In other extremes, might I wish to fictionalise what I have found, and to tell the story of the events from what I might believe to be the contemporary perspective of a person involved, whether real or imaginary?

Sharing your stories

There are many ways to present your stories online, some of which have already been alluded to earlier in this book. For example:

- You may wish to employ a blog-based platform (p.37), and perhaps break down your stories into small, creative, serialised posts that encourage people to keep returning for more with the next instalment.
- You might wish to present such written stories within the notes sections of online-based family tree programmes (p.70). The people

attracted to read such stories will have already been lured to your tree by the possibility of a connection as flagged up by the tree itself, and may well be in a good position to be able to answer questions that you may wish to pose within your narrative account.

- You might wish to give a talk about your ancestor, and share their story through a webinar or conferencing-based platform to a select family group (p.43).
- You can write your story on a simple word-processing package, add images and then export the final result into a PDF document. Once the document is complete, you can directly email the result to a relative, or if it is a large file, perhaps host it on a cloud-based service such as Dropbox (p.55) and then send the relevant link to all who may be interested.

Projects that are larger or perhaps a little more complex may require a different solution, particularly if seeking to create something a little more permanent. The following are some additional methods for conveying your efforts to your readership:

i) Websites

Having your own family history-themed website can allow you to create an entire project online, with dedicated pages for individual family history groupings or individuals, which can be updated at your convenience. Both Wordpress.com and Blogger, discussed as blogging platforms earlier in the book (p.37), can also be used as a means to create a free website, with the blog page just one constituent part of that. There are many other platforms that can be used to create free websites at the drop of a hat, however, such as Wix (**www.wix.com**) and Weebly (**www. weebly.com**), which offer similar free 'what you see is what you get' templates, and requiring little to no technical expertise.

Each web page has its own dedicated URL address, which stands for Uniform Resource Locator, and which can be accessed on different desktop browsers such as Chrome, Mozilla Firefox, Microsoft Edge, Safari and Brave, or through equivalent apps on phones and portable devices. Some websites may not work correctly on different browsers, and as such, it may be worth having more than one installed on your home computer.

Many companies offering free-to-use websites will do so with some conditions, such as limiting the amount of space available for your requirements (e.g. for hosting photographs), providing some limited advertising on your site when it is live, and a requirement of the user to use a domain name that includes their company name as a part of the address. Upgrading your membership to a subscription package may provide further benefits, such as the use of custom domain names, the removal of advertising, and additional tools such as site search capabilities.

A useful tool to consider adding to your site is a guestbook, where you can engage with readers. Some platforms will offer guestbooks as part of a package, others may not, but may permit you to embed a guestbook from a third party into your platform using HTML code (short for HyperText Markup Language). There are many platforms offering free guestbook facilities, such as Bravenet at **www.bravenet. com/guestbooks**.

When it comes to creating your own websites, something to be very aware of is that web platforms do come and go across time. If you are perhaps a little more computer savvy, an alternative is to create your own pages and designs using HTML files on a software programme such as Microsoft Publisher, and to then find an internet-hosting platform on to which you can host your work. So long as you have saved backup copies of this file, you can relocate it to another host platform of your choice as and when required.

Whilst you may have backups of materials hosted online at home, accidents and disasters do happen whereby such materials can be tragically lost. A further way to preserve the content of a site for posterity, in addition to saving copies on a cloud-based platform (p.55), is to save a cached copy of each page on the Internet Archive's WayBack Machine at **https://archive.org/web**, although this will only work on sites which

Web pages can be saved on the Internet Archive's Wayback Machine site.

permit access to a web crawler (a software tool or 'bot' that automatically indexes web pages).

To save a page you simply type in the relevant URL (p.116) in the box marked 'Save Page Now' and then on the link marked 'Save Page'. You can save a version of a webpage on more than one occasion, which can also be a very handy way to document the evolution of a family story that you are compiling across time. To retrieve a cached version of the page, simply visit the home page of the Internet Archive at **https:// archive.org** and type in the URL of the page you wish to see into the WayBack Machine box at the top of the page, and click return. A calendar will appear showing the various dates on which the particular site was saved, with each date having a clickable link allowing you to see the site as presented at that point.

Whatever means you use to create a website, the next stage is to announce its existence. Social media platforms, as discussed in Chapter 2, are a very useful way to quickly announce the launch of a new website, whilst directory-based sites such as Cyndi's List (**www.cyndislist.com**) are also well worth contacting to ask for a free listing in the longer term.

ii) Self-publishing

For larger narratives, however, a further option is to perhaps self-publish a book and to make it available online to your prospective readership. There are many platforms available providing such a service. Lulu (**www.lulu.com**) is a commercial publishing venture which provides options to self-publish both print- and e-book-based offerings. As well as providing a free ISBN number for your publication, the site offers guides and expertise on how to upload your written work, how to market it, and how to price it (including an option to make it available for free). An alternative is Kindle Direct Publishing (**https://kdp.amazon.com**), which allows you to make your book available for sale through Amazon (**www. amazon.co.uk**).

When self-publishing, the platform selling your work will usually not charge you to add your work, but will instead take a commission from each sale that is made. There are many advantages and disadvantages to using such sites. On the one hand, you will need to spend a considerable amount of time thinking about how to design such a book, with elements such as a cover and illustrations to consider (including their copyright status, p.15), and whether you need to learn a new text-based format, such as how to create an EPUB file (Electronic Publication; .epub) and to edit the elements within.

At the same time, by making your work available to purchase on such a site you will have a potentially much larger distribution network, although the commission you pay to the platform concerned might also reflect this.

Audio-visual

In addition to writing, we can also convey the stories of our ancestral past through audio-visual content presented online.

There are many forms of programming on the television and the radio which focus on family history, including the long running TV series *Who Do You Think You Are?*, of which there are many versions around the world. Desirable as it might be to produce a version of such a show to present our own family narratives, as everyday genealogists we are never going to be able to replicate the methods by which such programming is brought to life by professional broadcasters – and trust me when I say that, it was hard enough trying to achieve such productions when I had to do it for a living! As well as the immense financial cost to produce them, they also require substantial investment in time and effort to pull together.

Nevertheless, there are many ways that you can utilise audio-visual platforms to create online content to help share your expertise or to tell a story, and at next to no cost.

By whichever means you choose to share your content, you will need to first bear in mind several important issues.

- You will need to make sure that whichever device you are using to record your piece has enough storage, and that if needs be, you can easily export the recording to another platform for editing or display.
- You also need an ability to use the recording device – it is not always as easy as it looks on TV! For example, if you point a camera to record a conversation with someone seated in front of a window, and you are using your camera on an automatic setting, it will try to set its exposure based on the overwhelming bright light from the window, and in the process turn the person you are trying to record into a mere silhouette in the middle of your frame. Similarly if you are trying to record sound, the quality of the recording may well be diminished by background noise if you do not have a directional microphone.
- If you wish to use photographs or images, and/or music for your package, you will need to make sure that you have the relevant clearances to do so (see p.15 for more information about copyright).

- If recording whilst out and about, you will need to make sure that you have the relevant permissions to do so, if the area where you wish to do so is on private land. This might involve a simple courtesy call or written communication asking an owner if it is OK to proceed, but for more commercially based premises you might be asked to comply with more formal requirements, including a demand for a facility fee for the privilege (in which case a handy Plan B could be to your advantage!). When recording in a public place such as a street, there may be further considerations to be aware of, such as issues with filming children without parental consent, or showing details such as car number plates, which could potentially invade someone's privacy if you then upload your recording online without masking them.

The following are just some of the platforms for hosting audio-visual content online:

i) Video platforms

Family historians use video-hosting platforms for a variety of reasons: to look for historic film footage, lectures and presentations that may have been uploaded by archives, libraries and professional speakers: video tours to demonstrate key website features or genealogy techniques: for 'vlogging' (video blogging), and to simply find basic interviews or pieces to camera recorded by individuals to tell a story.

YouTube (**www.youtube.com**) is a video-hosting platform owned by Google, which allows you to freely host content on your own channel, and to watch other people's contributions whilst on the move using your mobile device or laptop, or in the comfort of your own home, via a desktop computer or even your own television set.

Another video-hosting platform is Vimeo (**https://vimeo.com**), which provides a free basic package offering 500MB upload capability per week, with various paid subscription levels offering further storage and functionality.

On YouTube, you can provide a description of the video, including links to websites which may be of interest, and viewers can also leave comments through a text-based comments facility under the video clip. Your channel can also be set up as a private channel to which only select individuals are given access. Videos can also be shared by email, by social media links, or an 'embed' code copied and used on a blog – this is essentially a link to the video in HTML format (p.117), which can be added to the code of a blog post or website.

Be your own broadcaster! YouTube works best with short clips, for easy consumption by viewers on the move.

It can be relatively easy to put together presentations using simple video editing packages on your computer, and to then upload to social media or to a video-hosting platform. If using a Windows 10-based PC, for example, the Photos app comes with an option to create a basic video presentation, in which you can add photographs and video clips, complete with zooms, pans and tilts, and on to which you can overlay music or commentary. There are also various inexpensive software programmes available to facilitate more creative editing techniques.

Alternatively, if producing a slide presentation on a programme such as Microsoft PowerPoint, you can record a narration directly on to the slides and then export the entire presentation as an MPEG-4 (.mp4) or Windows Media File (.wmv). Once you have the video file, you can then upload it to the relevant platform and advertise its presence through social media channels or by other means.

I am a big fan of YouTube, and on my own video channel will occasionally post short videos to promote books or courses that I might be doing, but I will also use it to share updates on genealogy lecture tours or to share stories from my own past. The following are a couple of examples:

Edwin Fox   https://youtu.be/K7e1V3vY8G0

On a visit to Picton, New Zealand, in 2011, I visited the last convict shop known to exist 'Down Under', the Edwin Fox. This short video diary both below the ship and on board it conveys a sense of the environment which convicts had to endure whilst travelling to Australia.

**In Search of the Mount
  Stewart murderer**   https://youtu.be/FZ49buVPp_I

Whilst writing a book in 2011 about the unsolved murder of my three times great-grandmother in 1866, I made a location recce to Forgandenny, close to the scene of the crime. In this short four-minute video diary I have just stumbled across the ruins of the house of the person who was accused of killing her.

As you will see from both of these examples, there was no budget, just me at a location, with a camera, and with something to talk about! When these were recorded, I used a small camcorder and uploaded the content to YouTube from my PC, but today content can be recorded directly through a phone's basic camera app and instantly uploaded to the platform through its sharing tools, or indeed to other social media platforms.

ii) Audio platforms
If you prefer the spoken word as opposed to watching video, there are many genealogy-themed podcasts accessible online, which are in essence pre-recorded radio shows. A podcast is essentially a file that can be listened to through a browser or downloaded to a portable device for listening whilst on the move.

Some podcasts are slicker than others in their production values, with the more professionally produced shows including Lisa Louise Cooke's *The Genealogy Gems Podcast* at **https://lisalouisecooke.com/podcasts**, with its mix of interviews and features, and the UK National Archives' podcasts at **https://media.nationalarchives.gov.uk**, featuring history and family-history-themed recorded lectures. However, any recording can be just as fascinating to listen to if it has something worth saying. Most podcast platforms will have their own dedicated websites, and you can subscribe to your favourites using a feed reader (p.43).

Basic audio recording is very simple, with most phones and portable devices including an inbuilt microphone and the relevant apps for recording sound, whilst file sharing apps such as Evernote (p.58) can also be used to gather sound recordings and to share them to a cloud-based storage facility for access elsewhere (p.55). These tools are very convenient for gathering sound, but with little by way of controls in terms of setting sound levels – if recording in a loud environment, for

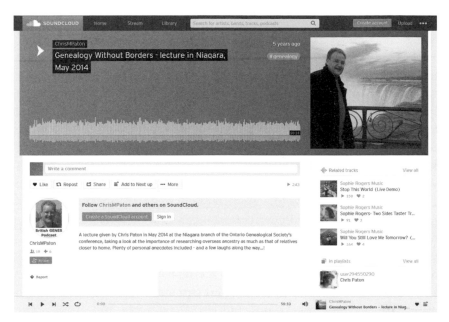

Soundcloud is one of many popular platforms for hosting genealogy-themed podcast recordings.

example, you may find that the device has an inbuilt limiter that 'crushes' the quality of the sound.

When recording audio on a home computer, you may find further flexibility in being able to set your own audio levels and with the editing of content. There are many sound editing programmes available online that can be downloaded for free, with one of the most popular being Audacity (**www.audacityteam.org**), which is a free open source programme that allows you to produce recordings with more than a single track, for example, with a voice recording on one track and music on another.

As with video, there are several online platforms for hosting audio recordings, with one of the most popular being Soundcloud (**https:// soundcloud.com**).

Further resources and advice for prospective podcasters can be accessed at Cyndi's List (**www.cyndislist.com/podcasts/general/**) and Geneabloggers Tribe (**https://geneabloggers.com/resources**).

FamilySearch Memories
This final option is one that certainly ticks many boxes on the multimedia front. FamilySearch Memories, a section of the FamilySearch website, accessible via the main menu or directly at **www.familysearch.org/**

photos, allows you to create a form of living time capsule of photos, stories, documents and audio recordings, by way of a digital scrapbook.

Content is freely stored in FamilySearch's digital vaults, and is hosted within a user's 'Memories Gallery', which is publicly accessible, within which items can also be tagged so that they can be placed with individuals on a user's family tree on the site (p.84). Digital images and audio recordings can be uploaded through the main website on a home computer, or through the dedicated FamilySearch Memories app or FamilySearch Family Trees app for phones and other portable devices. This is particularly handy if you wish to record relatives talking when you are out and about, with a guide on how to do so available at **www. familysearch.org/blog/en/familysearch-apps-oral-histories**. Recordings through the app can be up to a maximum of fifteen minutes in length.

Within the 'Memories' section of the FamilySearch site, you can click on the 'Gallery' menu item to access the relevant storage panel. In this you can create albums, into which you can store content grouped into individual sections for Photos, Stories, Documents and Audio. The platform will save materials in a variety of file types, supporting .jpg, .tif, .bmp, .png, .pdf, .mp3, .m4a, and .wav files, up to a maximum of 15MB in size. At the time of writing, video file imports are not facilitated.

A wonderful feature of Memories is the fact that you can add audio recordings to photographs within your Gallery albums, up to five minutes in length. This is a particularly great method for prompting memories from relatives, particularly for older relatives, who can see the event before them to encourage their recall.

FamilySearch Memories allows you to record sound alongside individual images.

In order to make a recording, simply click on the name of the photo of interest, and a new screen will be presented which will allow you to append additional information about the event depicted, including where and when it was taken, and to tag the image both for the person or people shown, but also topics of interest. Directly under the photograph, however, you will also see an image of a microphone with the words 'Record a Memory'. Make sure that your microphone is connected, and then click on the link – a new page will appear with an enlarged version of the photograph.

On the right-hand side of the screen, a large blue button is shown with an image of a microphone and the word 'Start', under the words 'What do you remember?'. Before you click the button to record, speak into your microphone, and as you do, you will see a darker circle of blue within the light blue circle rapidly changing shape as you talk. This is actually showing you your recording level; if you speak louder, the dark blue circle will grow, and if you speak more quietly it will shrink. So long as something is happening, it is picking up your voice, and you are now ready to record.

Now click on the word Start – the words 'Get Ready' will briefly flash up, and then a countdown from 3 to 1 will commence, at which point you can start to talk. You can pause the recording and continue at any stage. When finished, click on the 'Done' button, and you will then be returned to your previous details page, but now with an audio timeline displayed beneath your image. If happy with the recording, return to the main memories page, but if unhappy, you can delete the audio clip and start again.

Hours of fun!

FURTHER READING

ANNAL, Dave, and COLLINS, Audrey (2012) *Birth, Marriage and Death Records: A Guide for Family Historians.* Barnsley, Pen and Sword Books Ltd.

BETTINGER, Blaine (2019) *The Family Tree Guide to DNA Testing and Genetic Genealogy (2nd edition).* USA, Family Tree Books.

BLANCHARD, Gill (2014) *Writing Your Family History.* Barnsley, Pen and Sword Books Ltd.

CLARKE, Tristram (2011) *Tracing Your Scottish Ancestors – The Official Guide (6th ed).* Edinburgh, Birlinn Ltd.

FOWLER, Simon (2011) *Tracing Your Ancestors.* Barnsley, Pen and Sword Books Ltd.

GRENHAM, John (2019) *Tracing Your Irish Ancestors (5th edition).* Dublin, Gill and MacMillan Ltd

HERBER, Mark (2005) *Ancestral Trails.* Sparkford, Sutton Publishing Ltd

HIGGS, Edward (2005) *Making Sense of the Census Revisited.* London, Institute of Historical Research/National Archives

HOLTON, Graham (editor) (2019) *Tracing Your Ancestors Using DNA.* Barnsley, Pen and Sword Books Ltd.

JOLLY, Emma (2007) *Family History for Kids.* UK, Pymer Quantrill Publishing.

JOLLY, Emma (2020) *A Guide to Tracing Your Family History using the Census.* Barnsley, Pen and Sword Books Ltd.

PATON, Chris (2019) *Tracing Your Irish Family History on the Internet (Second Edition).* Barnsley: Pen and Sword Family History.

PATON, Chris (2019) *Tracing Your Scottish Ancestry Through Church and State Records.* Barnsley: Pen and Sword Family History.

PATON, Chris (2020) *Tracing Your Scottish Family History on the Internet.* Barnsley: Pen and Sword Family History.

SHRIMPTON, Jayne (2014) *Family Photographs and How to Date Them.* Newbury, Countryside Books.

SHRIMPTON, Jayne (2020) *Fashion and Family History.* Barnsley, Pen and Sword Family History.

TATE, W.E. (1983) The Parish Chest. Chichester, Phillimore & Co. Ltd.

INDEX